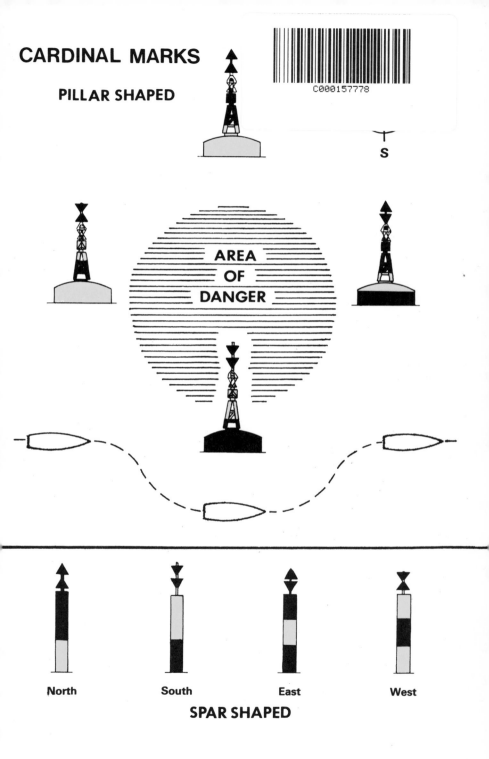

CARDINAL MARKS

PILLAR SHAPED

S

AREA OF DANGER

North   South   East   West

SPAR SHAPED

The Concise Competent Crew Guide

A study and revision aid
for the
RYA Competent Crew course

by

Howard Cheadle

David & Charles

This book is dedicated to all those friends on the East Coast who kept me going when I first started coastal sailing and made rather a large number of mistakes. And to all those who have suffered me as Skipper over the ensuing years, especially those Competent Crew who have had the misfortune to be instructed by me. I suspect I have gained far more from their company than they have from my instruction.

A David & Charles Book

© Howard Cheadle 1994
First Published 1994

Howard Cheadle has asserted his right to be identified as author of this work in accordance with the Copyright, Designs and Patents Act 1988.

A catalogue record for this book is available from the British Library
ISBN 0 7153 0193 4

Typeset by Creative Publicity Newton Abbot Devon
and printed in England by The Bath Press
for David & Charles Brunel House Newton Abbot Devon

About the Author

Howard Cheadle is a member of the Yachting Journalists Association, was for two years Features Editor of Yachting Monthly magazine and is a qualified and practising Yachtmaster Instructor. He now resides in Devon where he is involved in many aspects of sailing both afloat and ashore. He instructs on a regular basis with Plymouth Sailing School, whilst pursuing a career in yachting journalism and publishing ashore. His business, Creative Publicity, specialises in the design, illustration and typesetting of sailing books.

Although he has raced, he is a committed cruising sailor and, apart from exploring the UK coastline, has sailed and written about sailing in the Baltic, the Mediterranean and The Canary Islands.

His own boats have included a Contessa 32 and Sterling 28, one of the unsung classics from the drawing board of Holman and Pye.

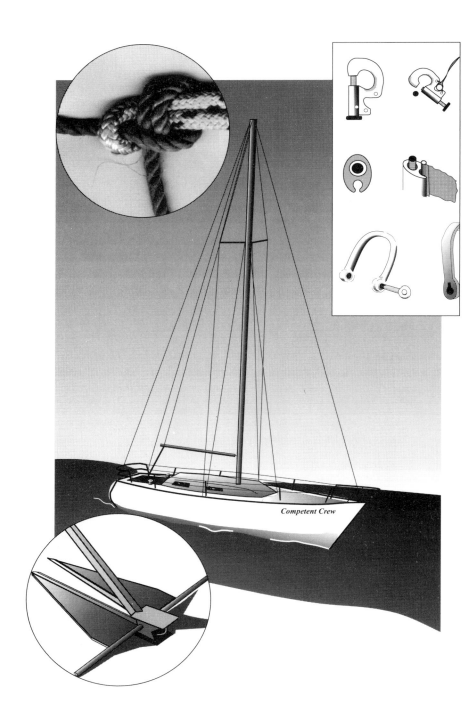

Competent Crew

Contents

INTRODUCTION

About Sailing...

If you have picked up this book in desperation looking for a gift to give someone, or perhaps simply out of boredom at a boat show, do not read any further. Why? Because you may just start to get interested in a pastime that has many happy addicts, myself included, and one which may change your whole way of life.

The image of sailing put out by the media is a confusing one. Sailing, particularly yacht racing, is often portrayed as being the pastime of the indecently wealthy, strutting about using sailing as a means of demonstrating their wealth. Sometimes sailing is portrayed as an outward bound adventure involving great hardship and danger, only for the brave and physically fit. Both these types of sailing exist but they are extremes. Every weekend throughout the summer millions of ordinary people take to the water in everything from home made dinghies to small yachts and quietly have a great time.

Sailing may be pursued as a casual pastime or, an active sport, or it may be an essential element of one's lifestyle. Part of its almost universal appeal is that sailing contains so many different opportunities for enjoying oneself. The young, and would-be young, tend to like the thrill of racing and for them getting wet, cold and occasionally frightened is part of the excitement. For those with more years behind them, cruising opens up opportunities for quiet relaxation, for making new friends or for finding solitude. Sailing has so many technical facets that hours of enjoyment can be had developing particular skills, be it in navigation, sail trimming, even boat maintenance.

But I am sure the key to why so many of us find sailing such a life-enhancing pastime is that it puts us in direct contact with our natural environment. You need know nothing about hydrodynamics, wave oscillations, or the physics of weather to take to the water and enjoy yourself. The magic of sailing is that when you hoist a sail, you catch onto the coat-tails of the wind and move. There is no engine other than that of nature driving you along.

I have been involved in sailing for thirty years or more, but whether in a dinghy or ocean going yacht I still experience the same excitement that moment when the sails are hoisted and, as if by magic, we start to move. Of course the pleasure does not end there; that is just the start. There is the pleasure of trying to sail a boat well, of exploring new cruising grounds, of admiring the beauty in boat designs, whether modern racing machines or traditional working boats. However underneath it all is the simple, inescapable and unchangeable truth, that sailing is dependant on natural, not man made, forces.

About this Book... .

You need know nothing about sailing to read this book. It has been written on the premise that the reader has little, if any, experience of sailing, and understands none of the jargon. The language of sailing is rooted in our maritime past and as a consequence many of the terms used on modern boats now have little apparent meaning. This book contains enough nautical terms to get you started and they are all explained in a way you can understand without having any previous experience.

Many of the terms used are masculine – crewman, yachtsman and so on. This presents a problem to someone like myself who wishes to dispel the myth that sailing is a boys-only pastime. Despite the notable and well publicised achievements of individual sailors such as Tracy Edwards and Claire Francis, sailing undoubtedly has a masculine image. There should be more women involved in sailing: their numbers are increasing but they are often consigned still to a supporting role, rarely that of skipper. Many wives/girlfriends/daughters are sent on sailing courses, particularly competent crew courses, at the request of the 'Skipper', not from their own desire to learn more about sailing; and they arrive with a background of having been told that just about everything that goes wrong on board is their fault. A few days on a sailing school boat and they soon realise that perhaps it is not they that need the instruction as much as their skippers. They discover, perhaps for the first time, that a boat can be taken in and out of a marina and sails hoisted, without the need for shouting or amateur theatricals. Even more importantly, they learn that sailing can be fun. I have not provided an alternative for each masculine term used in this book but I hope you have got the message that, as far as I am concerned at least, sailing is a pastime open for all to enjoy on equal terms. What counts is skill and mental determination, not strength.

The Royal Yachting Association Courses

The term Competent Crew and the letters RYA need some explanation. The Royal Yachting Association is a bit like the AA or RAC. It is a voluntary organisation set up to look after the interests of those who take to the water for pleasure. It is funded by subscriptions and donations and has no connections with Government, other than to work for the interests of water users on certain Government committees.

The RYA promotes the sports of sailing, powerboating, and wind-surfing, but when doing so, always emphasises the need for participants to do so in a responsible manner, careful of both their own safety and that of others. This has led to the establishment of a training scheme for yachtsmen which covers everyone from complete beginners to would-be offshore voyagers. The scheme involves classroom training ashore and tuition afloat. For those that like to have their competence independently assessed, there are certificates awarded for the successful completion of each level of training. This training scheme is regarded as being amongst the best, if not the best, voluntary scheme in existence anywhere. The standards of the highest qualifications awarded are such that they have become recognised as semi-professional qualifications.

The training system for yachstmen is described in a small and inexpensive RYA book, called the RYA Logbook. A table taken from the logbook showing the different levels of qualification is included at the end of this book, but it is well worth getting a copy of the whole publication.

Everyone has to start somewhere and the entry level to this training scheme is Competent Crew. The aim of this course is to introduce complete beginners to the way of sailing a boat safely, and take them through to the stage where they can step aboard a yacht with a degree of self-confidence, and know they can be an active and helpful crewmember.

This book covers the Competent Crew syllabus and a large section of the shorebased course called Day Skipper/Watch Leader which is intended as the next step.

But sailing is not about sitting in a classroom and so this book has been written with the emphasis on the practicalities of sailing and I hope you will find it a useful companion afloat for several years ahead. Most of all, I hope it encourages you to take to the water and experience for yourself the special magic of sailing.

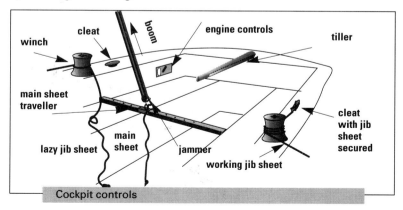

Cockpit controls

1
STEPPING ON BOARD

Stepping on board a yacht for the first time is an intimidating experience for the newcomer. Nothing is familiar; there are purposeful looking bits of shiny metal and rope everywhere. It all looks so mechanical and complex. And the language everyone is talking might as well be early greek for all the sense it makes. The only way to comprehend what everyone is talking about is to understand just a little bit about boat design and how a boat works. Fortunately, most boats conform to the same pattern, have the same basic equipment and are run in much the same way. There are a few designs, both modern and traditional that are a bit different, but 99% of all yachts follow the same principles.

Basic Boat Design

A boat has a *hull*, part of which is submerged, a *keel* or *keels* to provide stability and direction, a rudder at the back to steer with, and a mast to hang the sails on, and of course *sails*. There are lots of variations in the shape of hulls, keels, rudders, sails and the position and number of masts and sails, and these variations give rise to boats being called by different names. None of these names make much sense to begin with and there is no necessity to learn them all by rote. It may impress fellow crewmembers to be able to point out the difference between a *ketch* and a *yawl* but for our purposes it is far more important to know the basics of what to do practically, on any type of boat. To understand this we have to understand just a little of how a boat works; and as soon as you understand how a boat works, you will understand what some of the complicated looking bits of equipment are used for.

The Underwater Bits

Keels come in many guises; they may be described as short or long, deep or shallow, and a whole host of other names covering all sorts of peculiar shapes. There may even be more than one keel, although three is usually the maximum. A keel provides stability and stops the boat tipping over when the wind hits the sails. Dinghies tip over because the power in the sails overtakes the very limited stability offered by their lightweight keels. Keels on yachts are far more substantial and are designed specifically to prevent the yacht being tipped up so easily. Keels also play an important

9

part in being able to steer the boat as they provide some grip on the water and stop the boat just spinning round and round. Most keels are fixed and are of interest to us in running the boat only inasmuch as they affect the way a boat sails, how much water the boat needs to float (its draught), and what course of action to take should the skipper get his sums wrong, there is an embarrassing shortage of water and you touch the bottom (go aground). Some keels can be adjusted as to how much they stick down under the boat and can be raised, reducing the amount of water needed to float the boat, or lowered, increasing the amount of water needed but also increasing both stability and grip. They are often called *drop keels*, although the general idea is that you don't actually drop them off the boat, just raise and lower them.

Rudder A rudder is the prime means of controlling the direction of a boat. There is usually only one rudder, although you may come across twin rudders on lightweight racing yachts and catamarans. As with keels there are many variations in design. The rudder may be hung onto the back of the keel or have its own sort of mini-keel to hang off, called a skeg. The rudder can move from left to right and by moving it you steer the boat. It is operated from within the control centre of the boat, the cockpit, either by means of a long stick called a tiller or via wires and pulleys to the ship's wheel.

Holes Yes, believe it or not, a boat hull has holes in it. There may be several deliberate holes in a boat to get water into and out of the boat to cool the engine and work the toilet. These holes are called *water inlets* or

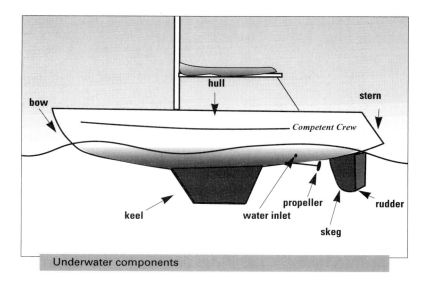

Underwater components

outlets. They can be opened and closed by using taps inside the hull called *seacocks.*

Engines A boat may have an *inboard* engine (usually diesel), that is an engine built into the boat, or an *outboard* engine (usually petrol) which is portable and is clamped to the outside of the hull. It is common to have a large inboard engine and a much smaller portable outboard for use on the boat's *dinghy* or *tender.*

Propeller With an inboard engine, there will be a *propeller* on the end of a *propeller shaft* under the water near the back of the boat. When the engine is running and put into gear the propeller spins and drives the boat backwards or forwards, but usually much better forwards than backwards.

I have set out a brief guide to the different types of hull, keel and rudder shapes at the back of this book should you find the subject of interest.

Above Water

This is where we need to get to grips with how a boat is sailed and learn some important sailing terms. It is blindingly obvious that we need to spread out the sails to catch the wind. We do this by holding them up using the mast. So let us look at masts first.

Masts Masts, usually made of metal or wood, are held up in place by wire ropes, just like a circus tent pole. The wires are called *stays*, because they help the mast to stay in position. The one going to the front of the boat is called the *forestay*, and the one going to the back, surprise surprise, the *backstay*. The ones coming down to either side of the hull are unfortunately called something completely different, *shrouds*. There are a few masts which are designed to stay up on their own and they are called *unstayed masts*. So far, so good. There are a few minor complications.

In order to widen out the angle the shrouds make with the mast, horizontal poles are fixed on each side of the mast called *crosstrees*. If a backstay can be shortened or lengthened easily whilst sailing, in order to adjust the bend in a mast, it is called an *adjustable backstay*. For additional strength a boat may have two backstays, *twin backstays*. The wire stays are connected to the boat by special adjustable metal fittings called *bottle screws*.

Some boat designs have, most inconveniently, backstays running to either side of the back of the boat which in certain circumstances have to be let go completely slack, called *running backstays*. The term *running* is an important one and will come up again; for running read movable.

Boom While we are looking at the large bits of metal we might as well include the *boom*. There is usually a boom attached low down to the back of the mast to hold out the mainsail and the sort of hinge fitting where it

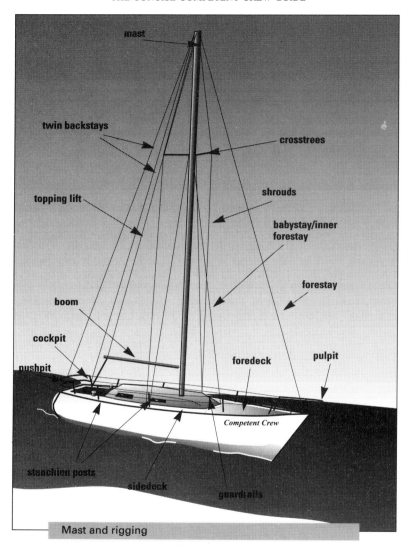

Mast and rigging

joins the mast is called a *gooseneck*. Occasionally the sail put up, or set, in front of the mast may have its own boom, but this is not common. There may be another pole attached to the *deck* (floor), used for setting a particular type of sail called a *spinnaker*, which we will come onto later. The pole is helpfully called a *spinnaker pole*.

If all this jargon sounds dreadfully complicated and you are already being put off, don't despair; when on a boat it is reasonably obvious what the bits of wire and metal tubes are for, even if you cannot remember the names.

Sails We have got our mast up, supported by its stays, so now we need the sails. Sails involve yet more jargon but once the basic pattern is established you will have no further trouble. Let's start with the sails at the front of a boat, the *foresails* or *headsails*. Most sails have a basic triangular shape. Each corner has a name, and each side has a name. The top is called the *head*, easy. The corner that attaches to the front of the boat at the bottom is the *tack*, you tack down a sail, and the remaining corner which points towards you when you are sailing is the *clew* – head, tack, clew. You must learn these terms. The side of the sail at the front and pointing forwards is called the *luff*, the bottom edge of the sail is called the *foot*, and the remaining edge the *leech*. You must learn these terms also.

Different size foresails have different names, none of which make any sense. The largest (other than two special sails we will come onto later) is the *genoa*. For a sail to be called a genoa or *genny*, the sail must be so big that when pulled back towards the cockpit, it comes back further than the mast. The next size down is a *jib*, and a boat may carry more than one size of genoa or jib. The most used size of jib is the *working jib*, the smallest a *storm jib*. Sails may also be further categorized by numbers, no1 jib, no 2 etc, the size going down as the number goes up.

We are almost there. The *mainsail*, the one attached at the back of the mast and to the boom, is also triangular in shape and it has exactly the same names: it has a head, a tack and a clew, a luff, a leech and a foot.

There are quite a few specialised sails but the two you are likely to meet are the *spinnaker* (sometimes called a *kite*) and the *cruising chute*. The spinnaker is a huge triangle of cloth which has a head and in effect two clews. Unlike all the other sails, it is not attached to the boat along any of its sides, just by ropes to the three corners. The cruising chute is slightly smaller, easier to control and conforms to the typical pattern of having a head, a tack and a clew, but again is set *flying*, meaning it is not attached to the forestay.

Hoisting the Sails

We have got the mast up, a boom and sails, what next? We need to attach the sails to the boat and then hoist them. With the foresails, one complete edge is attached to the boat, from head to tack, using either the forestay itself or sometimes a fitting around the forestay. With the mainsail normally two edges are attached, the luff to the mast and the foot to the boom. We will come onto how this is done later.

13

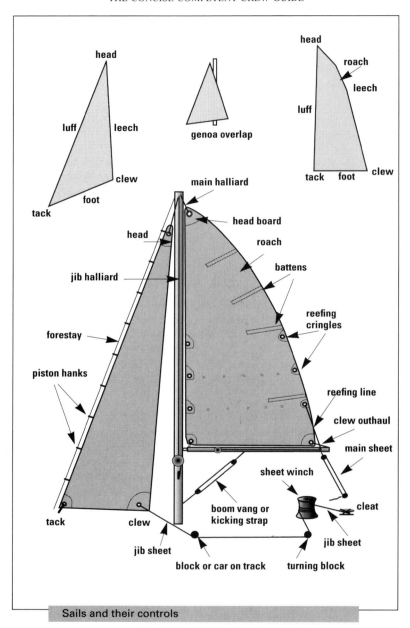

Sails and their controls

Now to put up our sails we need to pull their heads to the top of the mast. For that we need ropes called *halliards* (you h̲oist with h̲alliards). The halliards follow the names of the sails, so you have a *jib* or *genoa halliard*, a *main halliard* and a *spinnaker halliard* – easy. And if you want to raise a flag for having got this far in the most difficult, and boring, section of the whole book, you use a *flag halliard*.

Once having got our sails up into the wind it is no use them just flapping about, we need to be able to control them. And for this we use ropes called *sheets*. Say we have hoisted our jib, by first attaching the bottom corner of the sail, the tack, to the front of the boat, the luff to the forestay, then attached the top corner, the head, to our jib halliard and pulled it to the top of the mast there is only one corner left free to use, the clew. So we need to tie on our *jib sheets* (before the sail is hoisted!) to the clew in order to control the sail, to be able to pull the sail in tight or let it billow out just as we want. The sheets follow the names of the sails, so if we had hoisted a genoa the ropes would be called *genoa sheets*. We need two sheets for the front sail, each one going down opposite sides of the boat all the way to the back, so that we can drag the sail round from one side of the mast to the other as we don't want to sail in just one direction all the time. Confused? Don't be. I will explain this properly later and anyway one morning spent sailing and all will be clear.

The mainsail is hoisted in exactly the same way by attaching the luff of the sail to the mast, and the head of the sail to the main halliard, but there is no free corner. The bottom front corner, the tack, is tied to the front of the boom, and the back corner, the clew, is tied to the back of the boom. So where do we tie the *main sheet*? Well the only place we can attach our rope is to the boom itself. So the main sheet is tied to the boom and the sheet taken to the back of the boat.

Right! We have got the sails up, the sheets are tied to the sails and we want to go somewhere. We need to control what is going on and we do this from the back of the boat in the *cockpit*. Here we operate the three basic controls, the tiller or ship's wheel for controlling the rudder, the jib or genoa sheets for the front sail and the main sheet for the main. There are other bits of gear around the edges of the cockpit, and some inside, to enable us to handle these ropes safely (see diagram page 8). But you now have the basics of handling the boat: the jib sheets, the main sheet and the tiller or steering wheel, with the sails providing the power to move and the rudder to help control direction. With very, very few exceptions, step into the cockpit of a yacht ready to go to sea and you will be able to pick out these controls straight away.

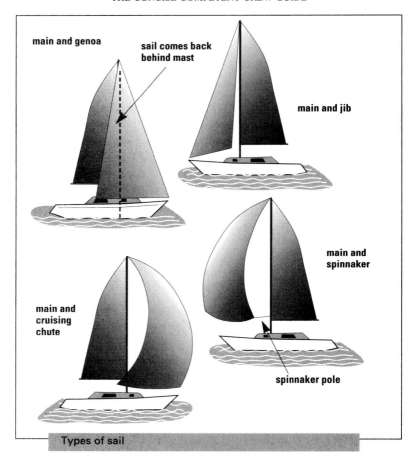

Types of sail

Accommodation

If the yacht or boat is big enough it will have some *accommodation* below, a sheltered space for eating, resting, navigating, hiding from the weather and telling tall stories. There are some unusual terms such as *heads* meaning toilet, *galley* meaning kitchen, *forepeak* meaning the narrow bit at the front, while beds are *bunks* and where you sleep is your *berth*; but there has been more than enough jargon for now.

It is time to sit down in the cockpit, relax and move on to something practical and much more fun, playing with bits of string.

2
ROPES AND KNOTS

L ife as a Competent Crew revolves around rope: pulling on it, letting it go, tying things on with it, tying the boat up with it, tying sails up with it. All day long just fiddling with bits of string. Usually that is why you are aboard, leaving the skipper free to do the fun job of steering, to shout abuse and generally indulge his fantasy of being an Admiral in Nelson's navy. He is also conveniently removed from being involved in any of the physical work. But he also knows that if he overdoes the abuse he may well end up joining the intrepid band of *single-handed* sailors, ie no crew.

We have already got some idea of the number of bits of string needed just to hoist and control the sails. To these we can now add all sorts of other bits of string; tying up the boat in harbour for example takes another four bits of string, each with their own names.

As life is to be dominated by string it is vitally important to learn early on how to handle rope safely and how to tie just a few knots, about eight in all.

Types of Rope

Rope has a fascination all of its own. There are many types and obviously many different sizes of rope but they all provide the same service in that, they can withstand a set force or load before they eventually break. And the loads on yacht lines can be huge as you will find out when you try and pull in a big sail in strong winds. There are innumerable ways of categorising rope and some of them are set out below:

Rope that stretches significantly when under load; rope that hardly stretches at all

Rope that floats; rope that sinks

Rope that is made by twisting one way, then another, individual very small filaments, called *laid rope*

Rope that is plaited, just like a little girl's plaits and called *plaited*, sometimes when more complicated *multi-plait*

Rope that is easy to handle; rope that is hard on the hands, or inflexible

Rope that resists sunlight; rope that is sensitive to sunlight and quickly loses its strength or degrades if left in sun continuously

Rope that resists rubbing and hard use; rope that is soft and easily damaged by rubbing or *chafing*

Cheap rope; very expensive rope, such as the special high strength/low weight rope found on racing yachts

Coloured rope

Nylon rope

Polyester rope

Polypropylene rope

Carbon fibre rope

Wire rope

The list goes on...

Rope technology has come on enormously in the last fifteen years or so and made life on board so much easier for all concerned. Rope is now stronger, easier to use and can be carefully designed to fulfil specific tasks. It is not just different sizes of the same bits of string.

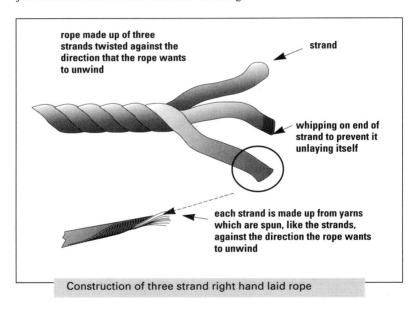

Construction of three strand right hand laid rope

Functions of Rope

We are going to look at ropes in terms of the functions they perform, starting with the two types of rope we have already come across, halliards for hoisting sails and sheets for pulling in sails.

Halliards They have to be strong enough to pull the sail up and keep it firmly in place for a long period of time. They also need to be not too thick or heavy, and they must be easy on the hands. Most importantly they must not stretch, for reasons which will become apparent later. Most halliards are therefore made of non-stretch or pre-stretched rope, sometimes laid, sometimes laid with an outer, softer sheath, sometimes plaited. Wire does not stretch and is very thin but it is heavy and is impossible to handle just using bare hands. However it is commonly used in halliards in conjunction with rope. The bit you pull on is rope and there is just enough rope for you to pull the sail up tight, but part of the line is made up with wire. The two are joined together with a *wire to rope splice*.

Sheets These must also be easy on the hands, they must be capable of withstanding very high loads without stretching, must be highly wear resistant as they are in constant use, and must be flexible. It is rare for sheets to be made up now with ordinary laid rope; on practically every yacht now you will find the main sheet and the genoa/jib sheets have an outer soft covering over an inner core. These ropes are immensely strong.

Mooring lines A new term, *mooring*, tying up the boat. Whether it be in the marina to a floating platform called a *pontoon* or to a *mooring buoy* (which is a big round float attached to the sea-bed by a *mooring chain*) mooring involves using a different type of rope. This rope must be able to withstand strong snatching or jerking loads, not just a continuous strain; does not need to be that easy on the hands but must be reasonably flexible, enough to be able to tie knots with it; and most importantly must stretch when placed under load. These ropes act like shock absorbers protecting the boat, the boat fittings and you, from sudden loads. They need not be small, can be laid or plaited but need to be protected against continuous rubbing or *chafing* if they are to be left in one place for any length of time. Fifteen minutes is quite long enough for a rough edge to saw its way through an unprotected mooring line.

Reefing and other lines Apart from the main ropes, the halliards, sheets, and mooring lines, there are a whole host of different uses for rope on a boat and each rope tends to get called by the purpose it is serving. When we reduce the size of a sail because the wind is too strong, we *reef*. There are different ways of doing this but they often involve using additional ropes called *reefing lines*. These are like the halliards and sheets in that they are non-stretch but can be much thinner than the sheets. When we lower a sail completely it seems a good idea not to let it blow all over the place, or completely off the boat, and so we bundle up the sails with *sail ties*. These may be made from anything providing it is flexible and does not damage the sail cloth. They can even be made up from 25mm (1in) wide lengths of strong ribbon-like material. Then there are bits of rope to tie down loose equipment, tie on to the handles of buckets (called *lanyards,* the rope that is, not the buckets) or tie on wandering children and dogs, called *safety lines*. Lots of jobs for lots of bits of rope. And therefore, lots of jobs to keep the crew amused.

And speaking of fun, now comes the best bit of the whole course, learning to tie knots. This can become obsessive, and there are plenty of books around to feed the obsession. Once you have learned the first eight required as part of the course, it is difficult to stop as there are hundreds of other ones you can learn, even ones you hope you never use such as a special knot for making up a set of stays and shrouds to hold up an emergency mast. And knots have such fascinating names, a Lighterman's Hitch, a Carrick Bend, a Cow Hitch; but I digress.

I cannot stress too strongly the need to learn the following eight knots. They will cover most eventualities. The ability to tie these without thinking is the greatest asset, apart from having a sense of humour, that a competent crew can have.

The Eight Basic Knots

If you can have someone with you who knows how to tie the knots and what the knots should look like when finished, this will help enormously. It is difficult to describe clearly in words how to form each knot but if you follow the instructions closely, take your time, and look carefully at the diagrams, noting in particular when an end of a rope goes behind or in front of another one, or down through or up through a loop, you will get there. Try and get the idea firmly fixed in your head of how the knot is made and what the finished knot should look like. The process of forming the knots as described will seem very clumsy at first but once you have got the pattern of each knot you will be able to make each one quickly and fluently in your own way.

You need two decent sized bits of string, about 1.5 metres long (about 5 feet), and not too thin; parcel twine won't do. It is worth buying a few metres of cheap sailing rope at a *chandlers* (a boat equipment shop). If the bits of rope can be different colours this will help, but it is not essential. Try and colour or mark clearly one end of each rope; the reason why will become apparent shortly.

A final piece of advice, tackle one knot at a time and stick with it until you are sure you have mastered it. Trying to learn all eight in one evening is not usually a recipe for success, only bad temper.

The Figure-of-eight Knot You need only one piece of string for this. The knot is classed as being a stopper knot, and as the name suggests the knot is designed to stop something happening. All you are doing is making a lump towards one end of your string to stop it going through some sort of fitting which has a hole smaller than the knot. The term figure-of-eight describes what the knot should look like when being made.

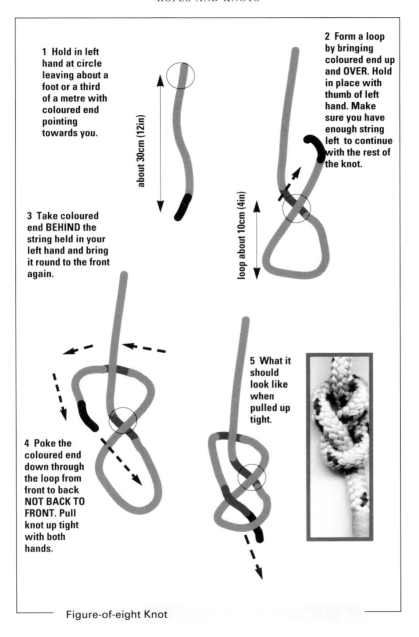

1 Hold in left hand at circle leaving about a foot or a third of a metre with coloured end pointing towards you.

about 30cm (12in)

2 Form a loop by bringing coloured end up and OVER. Hold in place with thumb of left hand. Make sure you have enough string left to continue with the rest of the knot.

loop about 10cm (4in)

3 Take coloured end BEHIND the string held in your left hand and bring it round to the front again.

5 What it should look like when pulled up tight.

4 Poke the coloured end down through the loop from front to back NOT BACK TO FRONT. Pull knot up tight with both hands.

Figure-of-eight Knot

Look carefully at the diagram. Hold the string firmly in your left hand (all instructions are for right-handed people), with your hand directly in front of you. You need to have about a third of the string pointing towards you (coloured end on your string, black in my diagram). Do not let go with your left hand until the knot is finished; it will feel awkward and when you know the knot well you can freely use both hands, but for now, do not let go. Form a loop about 10cm (4in) long by grabbing the coloured end with your right hand and passing it over the part of the string held in the left hand. Pinch the two strings together with the thumb of your left hand. Let go with your right hand. Stage one completed. Now, reach behind the length of string that is going away from you, grab the loose coloured end and bring it back round to the front and down through the loop. Pause and look at the shape; figure-of-eight, yes? Don't let go with the left yet. Pull on the coloured end while releasing the loop trapped under your thumb, but still keep hold of the string with your left hand. Pull the knot up tight. Figure-of-eight? If you have got it wrong you will most likely have tied an overhand knot which unfortunately won't do as it does not make a large enough stopper and is impossible to untie if pulled up tight. Look at the diagrams and start again.

Round Turn and Two Half Hitches This is one of the most important and useful of all the knots and is much favoured by professional sailors. It is easy to tie and easy to untie safely even when under strain, one of its most significant features; and it is secure. It is used for tying an end of rope around or to something, like the metal hoop of a *mooring ring* in a harbour or on top of a buoy, for tying lines to buckets, to poles, to *fenders* (sausage or balloon shaped plastic air-filled bags that are put out along the side of a boat to act as shock absorbers and to prevent the sides of the hull being scraped or damaged when coming in to a marina berth or alongside another yacht). Again you will need just one piece of string but this time something to tie the knot round, say a broom handle or back of a chair. In the diagram the pole is horizontal and in front of you. Hold the string in your left hand with at least half a metre (20in) pointing away from you, coloured end also away from you.

Stage one is very easy, just take the rope end in your right hand, drape it over the pole, let go with your right hand, bring your hand in front and underneath the pole, grab the coloured end and wind it over the pole again and let go again. We are putting on the round turn. Now for the two half-hitches. Bring your hand to the front and underneath the pole, grab the coloured end and bring it towards you. You pass the coloured end over the length of string still held in your left hand. Let go with the right, but hold on tight with the left using your thumb to hold one piece of rope on top of the other. With your right hand reach under the string held in your left hand, grab the coloured end and bring it upwards exactly as shown in the

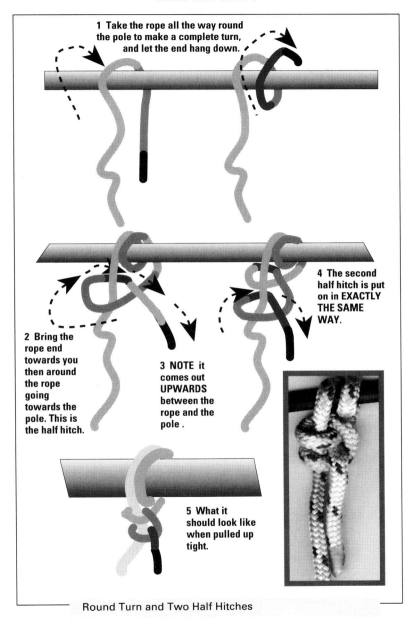

1 Take the rope all the way round the pole to make a complete turn, and let the end hang down.

4 The second half hitch is put on in EXACTLY THE SAME WAY.

2 Bring the rope end towards you then around the rope going towards the pole. This is the half hitch.

3 NOTE it comes out UPWARDS between the rope and the pole .

5 What it should look like when pulled up tight.

Round Turn and Two Half Hitches

23

diagram, nowhere else will do. OK:you have tied the first half-hitch. Now do exactly the same thing again and tie the second half-hitch. Pull hard on the coloured end to make the knot secure. Both hitches have to be made in exactly the same direction, otherwise you end up with what is called in the UK a *Cow Hitch* (the same knots have different names in other countries, many of the terms for useless knots being derogatory, eg an Englishman's knot in France is not meant kindly), and this is not anywhere near so secure. Got it, a round turn completely all the way round the pole, almost twice round in fact, then two half-hitches tied in the same direction. Master this knot and you can use it in an extraordinary number of ways.

The beauty of the knot is that although the rope that goes towards the ring or pole may be under tremendous strain, with care you can ease off first one half-hitch, and then the second, without the end you are easing off coming under great strain. A large part of the strain is taken by round turn. There is nothing more dangerous than a knot that cannot be undone quickly when you want to let go or *free off* a line in a hurry.

Clove Hitch This is such a simple knot to tie and yet many have the utmost difficulty in understanding how to do it. Same equipment as before, one line and a pole or chair back; and start in exactly the same way as before, rope in left hand, coloured end away from you etc. Take the coloured end over the pole and let go with the right hand. Reach round in front of the pole and pick up the coloured end, bring it upwards and over the pole again, crossing over the length of string still held in the left hand. Look at the diagram. We reach under the pole again with the right hand, grab the coloured end and poke it up in exactly the position shown in the diagram. Nowhere else will do. You must end up with the distinctive pattern shown, two loops on the outside, both lines coming away from the centre of the knot, with a line crossing over the middle. Sounds gibberish, but just keep looking at the diagram. If you get it wrong you will most likely end up with our friend the cow hitch again. It's such a shame it is not a more useful knot.

Now at great risk of confusing you, I will show you another way of tying the same knot. So far the pole has been horizontal. What if the object you want to tie onto is vertical, like a *bollard*, (short, often fat, vertical post found ontop of old-fashioned harbour walls) and you can easily place the knot over one end? Clove hitch Mark II coming up and something with which you can definitely impress other less talented crewmembers. Right, this time sit at a table. Lay out the rope across the table, coloured end away from you. Hold the rope in your left hand leaving at least half a metre (20in) to play with away from you. Grab the rope with the right hand about 15cm (6in) further along the rope, roll the rope away from you (clockwise) between your thumb and index finger, and bring your right hand to meet your left. You have just rolled a loop in the rope, yes? Pin the loop in place

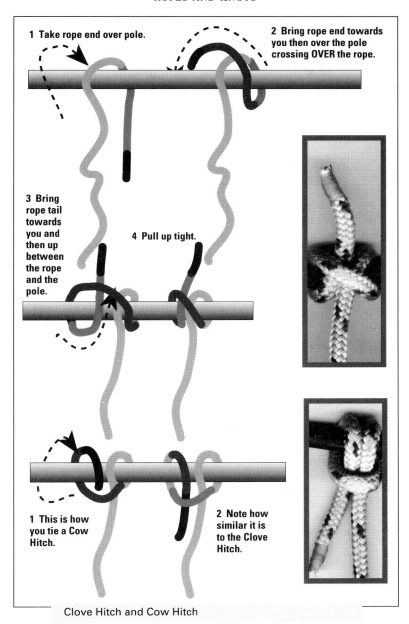

1 Take rope end over pole.

2 Bring rope end towards you then over the pole crossing OVER the rope.

3 Bring rope tail towards you and then up between the rope and the pole.

4 Pull up tight.

1 This is how you tie a Cow Hitch.

2 Note how similar it is to the Clove Hitch.

Clove Hitch and Cow Hitch

25

with the thumb and fingers of the left hand, and do the same trick again with the right, only this time slide the SECOND loop UNDER the first. Hey presto, a clove hitch ready to be dropped over a post or mooring bollard. Just do it casually, drop it over the bollard, pull it up tight and see the looks on the faces of your fellow crew.

A clove hitch is used for tying rope to poles, rings, and other ropes, fenders on to the boat, dinghies to mooring rings and bollards etc. It is less secure than a round turn and two half hitches and can be shaken loose accidentally. It is very quick to tie and as such is an ideal temporary knot. If it comes under continuous heavy load it can be very difficult to untie. You will use this knot over and over again, so keep practising.

Bowline One of the most famous knots, a very important knot, and one you must be able to tie without thinking. Its purpose is to form a loop in the end of a rope and is used for example in tying the sheets on to the jib or genoa, which means if you get it wrong it can be a bit embarrassing. The sail goes up, fills with wind and then the sheet drops off: not very impressive. If you are still sitting at the table, then this is a good place to try out the knot. Lay the rope across the table, coloured end towards you. Grab round about the middle of the rope with your left hand held out well in front. Right, now grab the rope with your right hand about 20cm (8in) closer than your left. Roll a loop in the rope in exactly the same way as with the clove hitch Mark II and trap the loop under the thumb of the left hand. Now for the confusing bit. Grab the coloured end with your right hand and poke it up through the loop. Now take the coloured end behind the length of rope going away across the table. All you have to do now is bring the coloured end round to the front again and back down through the loop. Look at the diagram again, up through the loop, round the back, down through the loop again. Finally grab the coloured end and one side of the loop in your right hand and pull really hard with the left hand on the rope that is going away from you. Unless you pull the knot up tight it will not work. Once you get familiar with the pattern, you will be able to tie the knot easily using both hands more fluidly but first get the pattern in your head. You can tie this single-handed when you get more fluent with rope, but don't even try this until you fully understand how the knot is made using both hands.

You are constantly wanting to form loops in the ends of rope, or through other rings or loops on a boat and hence the importance of this knot. It withstands very heavy loads, is secure under most conditions and can be undone relatively easily, but not if it has been under strain for a very long period. Most importantly the loop stays the same size, and doesn't slip, and so fortunately cannot be used as a noose should you severely upset the skipper.

Sheet Bends Not a diver's disease, just a very useful type of knot. Now we

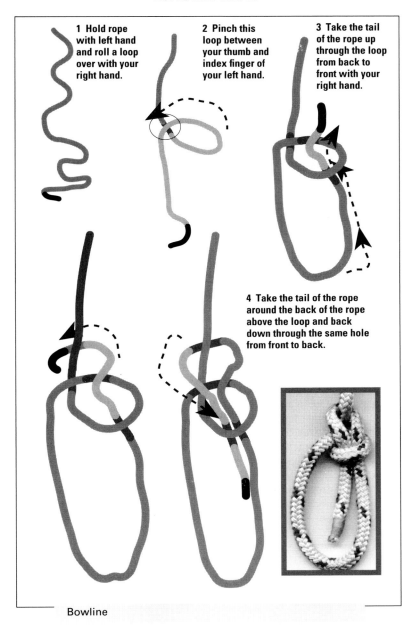

1 Hold rope with left hand and roll a loop over with your right hand.

2 Pinch this loop between your thumb and index finger of your left hand.

3 Take the tail of the rope up through the loop from back to front with your right hand.

4 Take the tail of the rope around the back of the rope above the loop and back down through the same hole from front to back.

Bowline

27

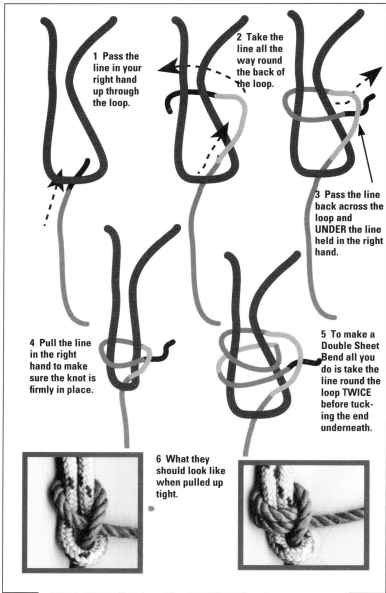

1 Pass the line in your right hand up through the loop.

2 Take the line all the way round the back of the loop.

3 Pass the line back across the loop and UNDER the line held in the right hand.

4 Pull the line in the right hand to make sure the knot is firmly in place.

5 To make a Double Sheet Bend all you do is take the line round the loop TWICE before tucking the end underneath.

6 What they should look like when pulled up tight.

Single Sheet Bend and Double Sheet Bend

need two pieces of rope. First tie a large bowline in the end of one of them. Yes I am afraid so, if you need to, go back one knot. First we will do a single sheet bend. This is simplicity itself. Hold the loop of the bowline in your left hand. Grab the coloured end of the second rope, poke it up through the loop from back to front, now take the coloured end round the back of the loop, bring it round to the front and tuck it under itself, not back down through the bowline loop again – that doesn't work at all. Look at the diagram. All you are doing is jamming the second rope against itself. Well if that is a single sheet bend, it will come as no surprise that a double-sheet bend has two of something. It has two turns around the loop, not just one. Look at the diagram. If you can tie a single sheet bend, then the double is no problem.

This knot has a very special quality. Where you want to quickly join a thin line to a thicker rope, then the doublesheet bend is the knot to use. Tied in an instant, much quicker than say a bowline, it can also be quickly freed. Providing tension is maintained on the lines, the knot, despite its fragile appearance, is unlikely to come undone. If it is to be left perm-anently tied, then the loose or free end has to be made more secure. Better still tie a bowline.

Only two more to go, one you already know from childhood.

Reef Knot One of the least useful knots, and one easily mistied. But it is useful occasionally and anyway it is part of the course. Use both ends of the same piece of string or better, both strings. Once again it can help to lay the ropes down on a table to see what is going on. This time the ropes cross in front of you rather than going away from you. Hold one rope in your left hand about 20cm (8in) from the end, with the end in front of you. Hold the coloured end of the other rope in your right hand. Simply twist round the rope in the left hand over, behind and then back in front of the rope held in the right hand. Stage one complete. This is where things go wrong. You take the end of the rope that started on the left, the coloured end in your RIGHT hand and do the same manoeuvre but in the opposite direction from right to left, twist the rope over, behind and then round to the front again (remember left over right then right over left?). Look at the diagram. You must end up with two interlocking loops, otherwise you have just tied a granny knot which is useless as it comes undone.

A reef knot is used, believe it or not, to tie up the loose bundles of sail cloth left when you reef (reduce) a sail. It is not one of my favourites, esp-ecially if someone does tie a reef in with it as it can be impossible to untie.

I have left to last a knot which is again very simple to tie, has a special and important function, but does take time to learn.

Rolling Hitch Remember the clove hitch? Have a practice, tie one end of your rope round the top of a chair. Now tie the other end round the top of another chair and stretch the rope out in front of you. Right, now we are

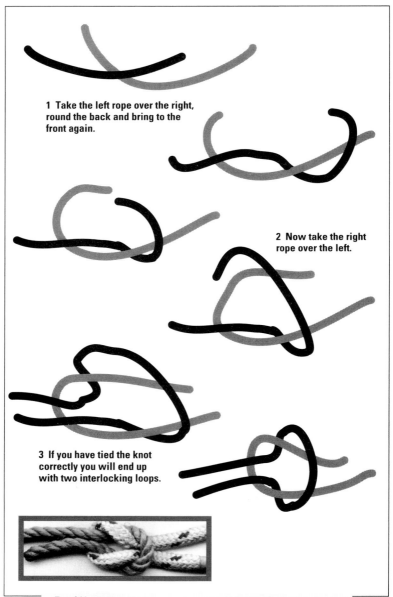

1 Take the left rope over the right, round the back and bring to the front again.

2 Now take the right rope over the left.

3 If you have tied the knot correctly you will end up with two interlocking loops.

Reef Knot

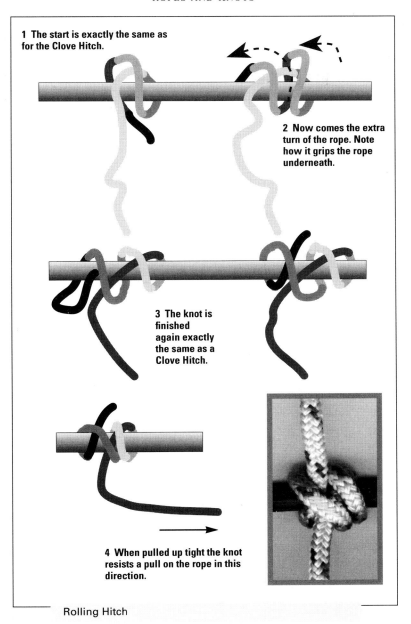

1 The start is exactly the same as for the Clove Hitch.

2 Now comes the extra turn of the rope. Note how it grips the rope underneath.

3 The knot is finished again exactly the same as a Clove Hitch.

4 When pulled up tight the knot resists a pull on the rope in this direction.

Rolling Hitch

going to tie a rolling hitch around this rope with your other bit of string. Start off the rolling hitch as a normal clove hitch by taking the coloured end of the rope over the top of the horizontal rope, back round to the front and over again, only do it twice, not once. Look at the diagram and make sure you have wound the rope around correctly with your right hand. Now finish off with a final turn as a normal clove hitch. Why the extra turn? The extra turn jams or nips the outside rope tightly to the inside rope, so tightly that it does not slip along the rope when pulled in the direction shown, even when placed under a huge strain. Why this is so important will be explained later, but first make sure you can tie it.

Now we are ready for action, time to use some of our new found expertise in knots to get the boat moving by hoisting the sails.

3
GETTING READY

We are still in harbour and the skipper has asked us, the crew, to get the sails ready to hoist. Unfortunately the skipper is one of those who puts everything away when he has finished sailing; we are lucky he has left the mast up. He has asked first that the genoa be *hanked on*, the sheets tied on with bowlines and led *aft* to the cockpit, through the *blocks* taking care to ensure that the sheets are taken *outside everything*, and fed in between the upper and lower *guard rails*. We don't need to be told that we have to put in figure-of-eight knots in the ends of the sheets that come back to the cockpit. The sail has to be tied up off the *deck* for now and we need not attach the halliard just yet. Lots of new words, but nothing to get steamed up about.

Getting out the Foresail

First we pull the sailbag (looks like a big duffle bag) marked genoa out of the cockpit locker (under the seats in the cockpit; the seat lid lifts up and reveals a huge locker containing an Aladdin's Cave of sailing gear) and carry or drag the sailbag forward to the front of the boat, the *bow*, along the *deck* (the floor). The bag has a drawstring top and using either this string, or better still another line that may be attached to the bottom of the bag, we tie the bag to one of the *guard rails* (wires, running from the front to the back of the boat and supported periodically by upright metal posts called *stanchions*, a sort of metal fence around the boat) with a clove hitch, BEFORE we take the genoa out of the bag. Sail bags blow away very easily, especially out at sea. At the front of the boat there is a sort of safety cage of shiny metal rails called a *pulpit* (a similar arrangement of metal tubes exists at the back of the boat, the *stern*, called interestingly a *pushpit*).

Now comes the tricky bit. We shake out the sail from the bag trying to keep the sail from blowing all over the place and we need to find the three corners, the tack, head and clew. It really is embarrassing to hoist a sail upside down and it can easily be done, simply by mixing up the head with the tack; the corners may be marked with the words head and tack, but not always. It is easy to establish the luff, as running along its whole length will be evenly spaced metal fittings called *piston hanks*, hanks because they are used to hank on the sail, and piston because the hanks, which look like the letter P, have a part, the stem of the letter P, which opens and closes with a piston-like movement. Each one of these pistons has to be pulled back and the metal 'P' hooked round the forestay. Sounds complicated but

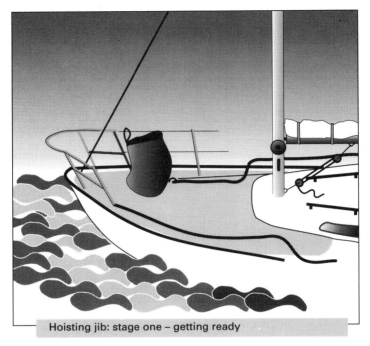

Hoisting jib: stage one – getting ready

obvious when you have to do it. We have found the luff, the head of the sail is usually much narrower than the tack so we are almost there. Where do we fix the tack to?

Fittings on the Foredeck

Follow the forestay right down to the deck at the bow and you will find several bits of equipment. Look at the diagram. Where the anchor goes out the front of the boat the deck and hull are protected by a U-shaped piece of metal, often fitted with a fat plastic roller, the whole lot called a *bow-roller*. The anchor may be left in place on the bow-roller but is often *lashed* or tied on to the deck nearby, or kept in a deck locker let into the *foredeck*, the area in front of the mast. Either side of the bow-roller will usually be other metal fittings that safely lead our mooring warps over the edge of the hull and deck, keeping the lines in place and preventing chafe, called *fair-leads*.

Two other bits of gear will be nearby. There is likely to be some fitting which ropes can be tied around. This may be in the shape of a small upright post with bars coming out each side, a *Samson post*, or an object

34

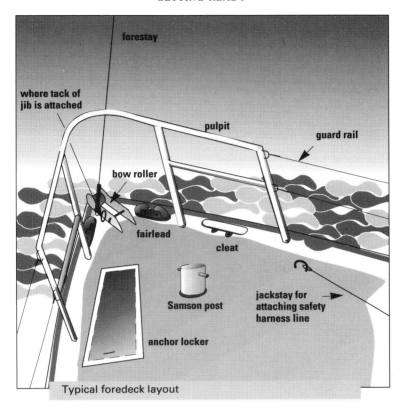

Typical foredeck layout

shaped liked two T's joined together, called a *cleat*, or perhaps a complex looking piece of machinery with a drum one side and rings with teeth between them on the other, called a *winch* or *windlass*. What we are looking for is a fitting right at the bottom of the forestay where it meets the deck. Here you will find another metal clip, called a *shackle*, a bit like the piston hank which clips on to the tack of our sail. This shackle may be on the end of a short length of wire, called a *strop*, not a strap. We attach the shackle to the tack.

Rigging the Foresail

It is good practice always to attach the tack first, it saves the problem of explaining to the skipper why his sail looks like a bag of washing and is half way up the forestay if we forget to attach the tack before hoisting the sail. Once we have got the tack attached we carefully clip on the piston

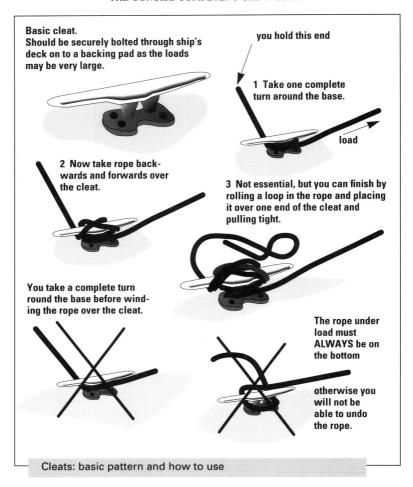

Cleats: basic pattern and how to use

hanks one by one in the correct order until we eventually arrive at the head of the sail, making sure as we go that the luff of the sail runs straight and is not doubled back on itself. We have only got one corner left now, so that must be the clew.

This is pulled along the *side deck* (floor either side of the boat running from the cockpit to the foredeck), not too vigorously as sails are expensive and can easily be torn by being snagged on a fitting. As the sail is pulled alongside the guard rails, we run our hand down the top edge, the leech, making sure that the leech runs in a straight line from the head of the sail

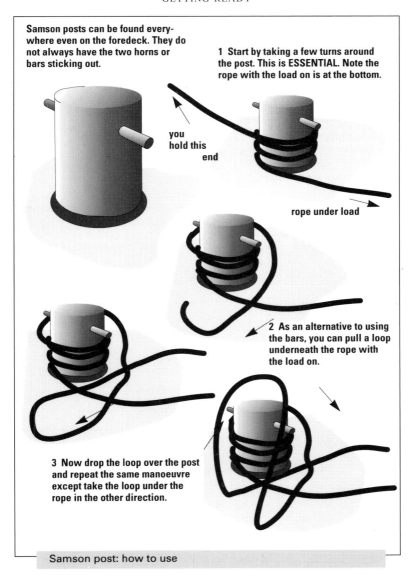

Samson posts can be found every-where even on the foredeck. They do not always have the two horns or bars sticking out.

1 Start by taking a few turns around the post. This is ESSENTIAL. Note the rope with the load on is at the bottom.

you
hold this
end

rope under load

2 As an alternative to using the bars, you can pull a loop underneath the rope with the load on.

3 Now drop the loop over the post and repeat the same manoeuvre except take the loop under the rope in the other direction.

Samson post: how to use

right to the clew and is not twisted. To stop the sail blowing away or getting damaged by being trodden on, we bundle it up off the deck and tie it on to the guard rails using *sail ties* (any bit of string). You can use a reef knot but do not pull it up tight as it will be difficult to undo unless it is *slipped*. What's this, a new knot, not on the list? Worse than that, a whole range of knots. A knot which is tied so that it can be quickly undone, usually just by pulling one end, is called a slipped knot; you can have slipped clove-hitches, sheet-bends, reef knots. Use a clove hitch for now and if it seems loose, tie the two ends together right over left.

The genoa sheets (two of them) are usually kept in the cockpit locker. Check with the skipper that you have got the right ropes, as the locker will be full of bits of string. Now attach one end of each sheet to the clew using a bowline. The *tail* or loose end of the knot must be long enough to allow the knot to be undone easily, so make it at least 10cm (4in) long, preferably longer. The size of the loop varies with skippers; I prefer the loop to be quite large, not less than 15cm (6in), others prefer much bigger or smaller bowlines. With the bowline tied on and pulled up tight we have to thread the sheet back to the cockpit. You will be quite close to the cockpit on the side that the sail has been tied off.

The sheet goes from the sail to a *block* or *pulley*, maybe more than one, then to the winch and the cockpit. The block is usually mounted on the

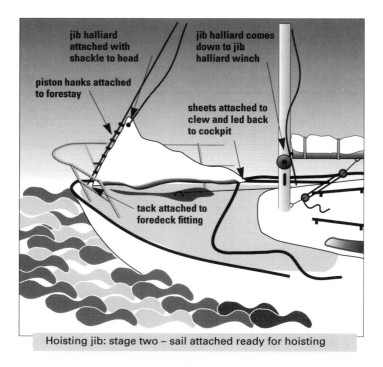

Hoisting jib: stage two – sail attached ready for hoisting

deck on top of a flat metal rail with holes in it. The idea is that the block can be moved backwards and forwards along this track to adjust the shape of the sails. We make sure that the sheet comes from the clew through the front of the block and goes towards the back of the boat, not the other way round. And remember the skipper has said he wants the sheet to go between the upper and lower guard rails; the sheet must do this before it gets to the block. So the line goes from the clew out over the top of the guard rail, back in between the two rails beside the block, through the block to the winch, all the slack is pulled in, the spare rope coiled over the winch and a figure-of-eight tied in the end. The same exercise is repeated for the other sheet except that this time it must be led right round to the other side of the boat. It is led inside the forestay, but outside all the shrouds. Look at the diagram which makes this much clearer. It is a common mistake to mislead the sheet lines, everyone does it at some time.

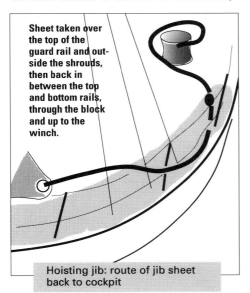

Sheet taken over the top of the guard rail and outside the shrouds, then back in between the top and bottom rails, through the block and up to the winch.

Hoisting jib: route of jib sheet back to cockpit

We have two last jobs, first we temporarily unclip the tack and pull it up off the deck to make removing our mooring lines much easier and we tie down the head to stop the sail creeping up the forestay until we are ready to hoist it; we can do both jobs with one long sail tie.

Rigging the Mainsail

All this work and we haven't even left harbour yet. Now for the main. It is unusual for the main to be taken off the boom ever time you finish sailing. It is usually left on all season and protected from the damaging effects of sunlight with a *sailcover*. However our skipper has had his sail repaired and it needs to be put back on again.

Remember, head, tack, clew. The head is the easiest to find as it has special stiffening in the form of a *headboard* which makes the top of the sail rigid. The luff is attached to the mast and the foot to the boom in one of two ways, either with small plastic runners, a bit like curtain runners that slide into a track or by having a rope sewn along the edge of the sail which runs along a groove. It is easy to get confused, so work out where the head is, then run down the edge that has the sliders or rope sewn along its length this must be the luff, and you arrive at the tack. As we have found the head and tack, the other corner has to be the clew. The sail is fed onto the boom first, starting with the clew, feeding it into the boom at the mast end and pulling the sail out along the boom. The tack and clew must now be attached, the tack first, usually with a thin or *light* line tied backwards and forwards many times through a hole or ring on this end of the boom. When the tack has been firmly tied on, then the clew is attached to a much stronger rope or even a wire fitting, called a *clew outhaul*. This rope is used to tension the foot of the sail and change the shape of the sail. It is a highly important rope. The clew outhaul will run either to a fitting at the back of the boom, or will be led through pulleys back towards the mast again, often inside the boom, emerging either through the side of the boom beside a cleat or right back to the mast where a jumble of ropes will be found leading out from under the boom – we will come on to these later. It is the skipper's job to tension this line, but you should make sure it is attached.

Right, the sail is fitted along the boom, we can now start fitting the sliders into the mast, starting at the head of the sail. There may well be a *gate* which stops the sliders falling out once they have been fitted in. It is all a bit fiddly and there is quite a variety of fittings used. If the sail has a rope luff, then you do not feed this in until you actually hoist the sail. We now have to tidy up the main and tie it along the boom. There are two ways of doing this: either the sail is *flaked* which means that equal folds of the sailcloth are draped over the boom, or a bag shape is formed by holding out the leech of the sail at the back of the boom, forming a long sausage-like shape running along the length of the boom, and stuffing all the rest of the sail into this tube. Whatever method, the sail has to be securely tied on top of the boom using sail ties.

Mainsail Lines and Gear

What about the main sheet? Look under the boom at the cockpit end and you will find a rope going backwards and forwards through pulleys to another track going horizontally across the boat. This track may be at the front of the cockpit, in the middle dividing the cockpit in two, at the back of the cockpit, or more rarely, on top of the boat in front of the cockpit across the *coachroof*. This track is called the *mainsheet traveller*. Fixed to

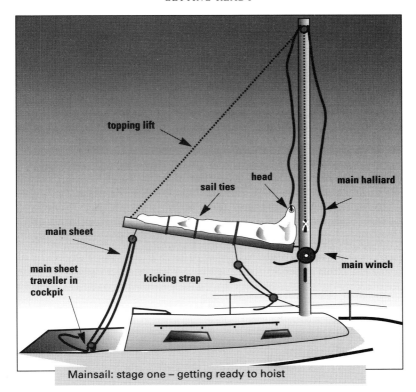

Mainsail: stage one – getting ready to hoist

the track is a large *block* (a collection of pulleys, all in line) and where the rope comes off the pulleys it is fed through a mechanism with little jaws, called *jammers*. You can pull the main sheet towards you through the jaws but when you let go, the jaws grip the rope for you. The strain on this rope and on the genoa sheets has to be experienced to be believed. There will be an enormous length of rope coming out of the jammers; this is the main-sheet and of course needs a stopper knot tied in the loose end.

While we are on deck hanging off the boom there are two other lines we can look at, one going from the cockpit end of the boom up to the top of the mast (and back down again otherwise we couldn't adjust it) which holds the boom up when a sail is not hoisted and is called the *topping lift*. The boom does not stay up all on its own defying gravity; without this line the boom would drop down onto the deck or onto fellow crewmembers' heads in the cockpit, so this line is not released until the sail is up.

There is another line under the boom, about a third of the way back

41

from the mast, which goes at an angle back to the base of the mast. This is called a *kicking strap* or *boom vang*. Again this has to do with sail trim and stops the boom lifting up in the air under certain conditions. Find out where the end of the rope is and how it is fastened because you may well be asked to *ease off* (loosen) or *harden up* (tighten) on the *kicker* when sailing.

We thought we had finished but the skipper has asked whether we put the *batons* back in their *pockets*. Batons (also spelt battens) are short flat sticks that tuck into sleeves made at intervals down the leech of the main. The idea is that they help support the area towards the back edge of the sail, called the *roach*, and improve the shape and therefore the power the sail can produce. A very modern development is the use of batons that reach from the mast right to the back of the sail, in which case the sail is described as having a *fully-batoned main*. We just have ordinary batons, each one a different size and we tuck these securely into the sleeves.

At long last we have the sails ready, it is a fine day, and the skipper is anxious to make the best of the weather. The engine goes on, and the skipper asks us to stand by the mooring lines and get them ready to *slip*, let go. A last look round, and we are off.

4
HOISTING SAIL

Right, we have successfully left harbour (how this is done will be tackled later) and tidied away all the fenders and mooring warps into the cockpit locker. The fenders may just get jammed in but the mooring lines must not just be thrown in and end up as a pile of spaghetti at the bottom of the cockpit locker. They have to be put away properly by being coiled.

There is great satisfaction to be had in doing this job well: it makes you feel like a proper sailor and does not take long to learn. If the mooring warp looks as though it is a laid rope (see diagram page 18) then you grab hold of one end of the rope in your left hand and form loose coils approximately the same size, in a clockwise direction. You will find that the rope wants to form a twist; you counteract this by rolling the rope between your thumb and first finger in much the same way as when you did the Clovehitch Mark II.

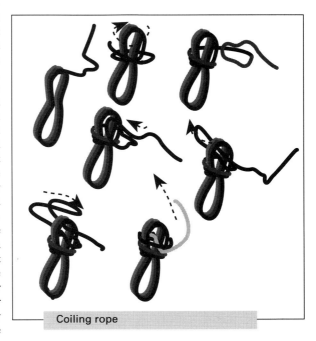

Coiling rope

When you have about 1.5 metres (5ft) to go, you bunch the coils in your left hand and wind the loose end of the rope around and around the coils. To finish off you push a loop, not the end, but a loop through the coils, pass the loop over the top of the coils and then pull on the loose end to pull this loop tight around the coils. If you have judged the length just right you will have enough rope left to be able to tie up the mooring warp to a cleat or other fitting in the locker. If the rope is plaited, when the coils form they take up a figure-of-eight shape which is perfectly all right.

43

Hoisting the Main

It is usual to hoist the main first. The skipper points the boat's nose into the *prevailing* wind (straight into the wind whichever direction it is coming from) so that as the main is hoisted the wind blows the sail back down the length of the boat, not across it which would make the sail impossible to hoist as it would get stuck under the crosstrees. First we find the main halliard which will be clipped off with another type of shackle somewhere

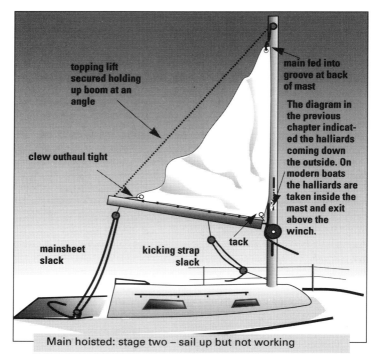

topping lift
secured holding
up boom at an
angle

main fed into
groove at back
of mast

The diagram in
the previous
chapter indicat-
ed the halliards
coming down
the outside. On
modern boats
the halliards are
taken inside the
mast and exit
above the
winch.

clew outhaul tight

mainsheet
slack

kicking strap
slack

tack

Main hoisted: stage two – sail up but not working

nearby. Convention has it that the main halliard comes down the right hand or *starboard* side of the boat as judged when looking forward from the cockpit. The halliard may be outside the mast, or inside it and coming out through a slot in the side of the mast called a *sheeve,* and then going to a winch on the same side of the mast, or may lead back from the bottom of the mast across the coachroof to a winch sited on top of the coachroof within working distance of the cockpit.

To hoist the sail we need to clip the halliard's metal fitting onto the head of the sail, take off the sail ties and pull on the other end of the halliard.

Simple. But before we hoist, we must first loosen off the kicking strap under the boom, and *free off* (let go) the main sheet, otherwise we will not be able to hoist the sail properly. The luff has to be pulled up very tight – the stronger the wind the tighter the luff – and for this reason, the halliard is led round a winch so that it can be pulled up really firmly. Before winches were so common the halliard was pulled up by hand and tightened by *sweating it up,* quite an apt term as it involved a lot of physical effort.

Once pulled up tight, the halliard is *cleated off,* that is tied securely round a cleat, and any loose rope coiled away in much the same way as the mooring warps except that this time the loop is not made from the loose end but by reaching through the coils to the part of the rope that is coming off the cleat, pulling a length of this through the coils, twisting it and then putting it back on the cleat. The halliard must be secure against slipping, which is what tying it to the cleat does, but it must also be ready to be let off quickly in an emergency, hence the different way of tying up the coils.

The sail is up and flapping, and the skipper asks us first to ease off the topping lift (which will usually be led down the same side of the mast as the main halliard) until the boom drops down and is held up by the sailcloth. The main sheet is then hardened in (pulled in) by the crew in the cockpit, the kicker tightened up by us up on deck and secured, and in those immortal words, 'we are sailing'.

Hoisting the Genoa

Unfortunately, our work is not yet done. Having put the sail ties we took off the main somewhere safe, we have to think about hoisting the genoa. Whichever side of the boat the boom is hanging over, we go up the other, and in rough weather we would crawl up on hands and knees. First, we take the sail tie off the tack and head and fix the tack to the fitting at the bottom of the forestay. Next we find the genoa halliard: let us hope the skipper will be sufficiently interested to say something like, 'it's the green rope tied on to the port side (left) of the pulpit'. The halliard is attached to the head of the sail with another special metal clip or shackle. We then wait until the sail is ready to go up, and only remove the sail ties holding the sail along the rails at the last moment. The genoa halliard conventionally goes down the port (left) side of the mast and like the main it can be led outside the mast, inside the mast coming out near the boom or be led back to the cockpit through more *deck fittings* (more or less anything securely fixed to the deck). The skipper gives the command to hoist, the sail ties are slipped off, and the sail goes up with the wind blowing the sail away from the boat and from us the able foredeck crew. The crew in the cockpit pull in on the genoa sheet once the sail is hoisted, and we go back to the cockpit, again on the opposite side to the boom. Nothing to it really. Just takes a bit of practice.

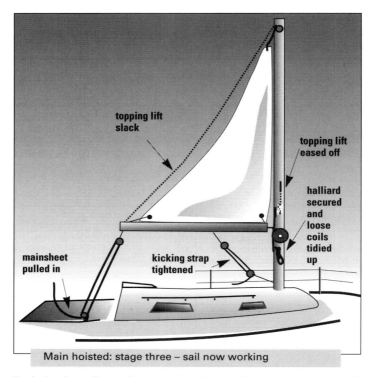

topping lift
slack

topping lift
eased off

halliard
secured
and
loose
coils
tidied
up

mainsheet
pulled in

kicking strap
tightened

Main hoisted: stage three – sail now working

To hoist the sails we have got involved with piston hanks, shackles, winches and cleats and we need to have a closer look at all of these.

Piston Hanks Piston hanks are as described in the diagram. They can be very difficult to open as the piston gets clogged with dried salt. They can also get damaged and bent. It is acceptable as a temporary emergency to miss off a couple of the hanks but the sails will not set so well. If you can't get one to open then tell the skipper. He may have the tools handy needed to unjam it (a pentrating oil such as WD40 and a hammer). It takes time to fit on all the hanks and at sea the bow is the coldest, wettest, most dangerous and most sea-sick making place to be. It is much better to get the sail hanked on in the flat calm of the harbour than in the sea outside the harbour walls. There are also other ways of fixing the headsail onto the forestay which we will look at later.

Shackles There is an enormous variety of metal fittings that get put on the ends of ropes, halliards, etc. The halliard will have a permanent loop formed in the end of it. The loop is called an *eye* and will have a metal lining called a *thimble*. The loop will have been formed not with one of the knots we have

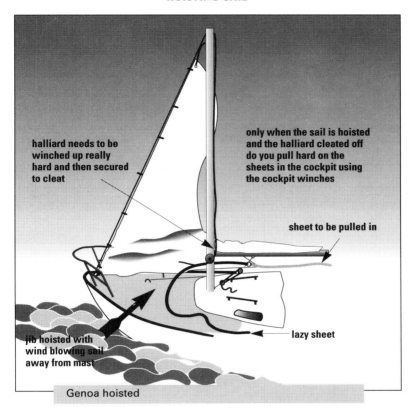

halliard needs to be winched up really hard and then secured to cleat

only when the sail is hoisted and the halliard cleated off do you pull hard on the sheets in the cockpit using the cockpit winches

sheet to be pulled in

lazy sheet

jib hoisted with wind blowing sail away from mast

Genoa hoisted

looked at – they are too bulky – but by being *spliced* (woven) back on itself and have *whipping twine* (very fine strong line, like thick sewing cotton) wrapped tightly round it. Through the metal thimble will be a shackle. The simplest of these is a metal U with the U closed off by a metal bar that is threaded at one end and has an obstruction at the other. (Look at diagram page 49.) To open it you unthread the metal bar called the *pin*. If it is jammed you need a *shackle key,* which is simply a piece of metal with a slot in the middle which gives you some leverage. Beware, the pin can come completely out. So if you are using one of these to attach a halliard to a sail don't lose the pin! If the skipper has any sense he will have purchased a shackle with a *captive* pin, that is one that can't fall out. The pin must be tightened up really hard before you hoist the sail.

Another common shackle is one where the pin has a bump on the side of it which has to go through a slot in order to secure the pin. This time you turn the pin round a half turn until it clicks into place.

Another shackle commonly used is a *snapshackle*. This is a variation of the piston hank. You pull a spring-loaded pin out one side and the shackle snaps open. You must make sure the pin is pushed fully home again before the sail is hoisted.

Winches The ability to handle winches safely is essential. The importance of using them correctly cannot be overstressed as used incorrectly, you are asking first, to damage your hands; second, to cause an accident to someone else on the boat, and third, to damage the boat itself. They are the easiest pieces of equipment to use, and become easier if used correctly. A winch is a metal drum, wider at each end than the middle, with gears inside it which connect to a removable handle. The *winch handle* is inserted into a star shaped hole on the top of the winch; you pull the handle round and round and it causes the winch drum to rotate. We need them because they greatly increase our ability to pull in lines. We can exert a tremendous pull on a line if it goes round a winch; it is like having a little engine at our disposal. If a rope, say a genoa sheet, is led to the bottom of the winch, then wound round the winch drum three times, the pull you can now exert on the rope by *grinding away* with the winch handle is enough to pull a huge sail in tight, even in a strong wind. To make matters even easier for us, it is common for the genoa winches to have two or sometimes three gears. You turn the handle round in a clockwise direction in first gear and when you have not got the strength to move the handle any further clockwise, you start rotating the handle anticlockwise. This engages second gear and makes life easier. The drum still continues to turn in a clockwise direction, but much more slowly. A winch with gears is described as being a *two-speed* or *three-speed* winch.

Without the winch you simply couldn't exert enough force on the sheet to pull it in. The rope grips on to the shiny metal of the winch by friction, particularly the friction of the rope against itself as it coils up the winch drum. The sequence for pulling in on a winch is always the same.

Stage one The line is led to the winch and is wound round once in the direction that the winch goes round, usually clockwise. This is easy to check, just turn the top of the winch in your hand.

Stage two All the slack in the rope is pulled in.

Stage three AT LEAST two more turns are put round the winch before the winch handle is put in the end. Now holding the rope coming off the winch pulled taut with your left hand, turn the winch handle round and round with your right, keeping the rope taut in your left hand all the time. If two people are available it helps if one grinds away on the handle whilst the other *tails* (holds on to the rope). Once the rope is in tight enough – the skipper will say when – then the rope coming from the top of the winch must be tied off tight and securely, usually round a cleat.

There is a modern piece of equipment that removes the need to tie off the

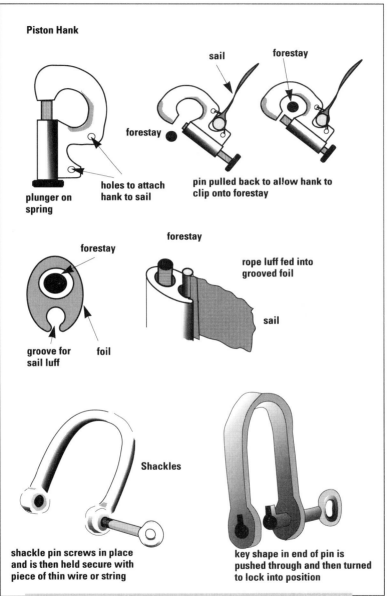

Piston Hank

sail

forestay

forestay

holes to attach
hank to sail

pin pulled back to allow hank to
clip onto forestay

plunger on
spring

forestay

forestay

rope luff fed into
grooved foil

sail

groove for   foil
sail luff

Shackles

shackle pin screws in place
and is then held secure with
piece of thin wire or string

key shape in end of pin is
pushed through and then turned
to lock into position

Piston Hanks and Shackles

line securely, called a *rope lock*, sometimes a jammer. In this instance rope goes through the jammer BEFORE it gets to the winch. Once the rope is tight enough the rope is *locked off*. This is not used on genoa and jib sheets but may be used on halliards, topping lift, kicking strap etc. Once locked off, the end of the rope can now be taken quite safely off the winch, freeing the winch up to be used for another line.

What if we want to let the rope off? Well remember it may be under the most enormous strain so it is not a question of just letting everything go with a bang, or else it might do just that. You carefully untie the rope from the cleat keeping a tension on the line between the rope and the winch. You let the coils of rope around the winch gently slip round, helping control the situation by pressing the rope against the drum with the palm of your hand. As the tension is eased out of the rope, then the coils can be removed quite quickly off the winch by pulling upwards and then letting go. It becomes second nature in the end.

Where a rope lock has been used, you must first tightly wind at least three coils back round the winch you used, BEFORE letting off the jammer, if the line is under strain.

That just leaves cleats.

Cleats Wonderful devices, so simple and yet often incorrectly used (see diagram page 36). The line coming to the cleat that is under strain, or is going to be under strain, is taken all the way round the base of the cleat once. That provides the grip and that is the bit most people miss out. You now form figure-of-eights, not knots, just loop the rope back and forward over the top of the cleat using the horns at each end. Three of these is ample. To finish off you may do a *locking hitch* over the top which does not add greatly to the security but stops idle hands from undoing a loose end left on the deck. Ask the skipper what he prefers you to do, as there is a great deal of controversy over locking off lines, particularly sheets and halliards, with the view expressed that such lines should never be locked off in case they jam and can not be undone in a hurry. You never tie a rope to a cleat so that the line with tension in it comes off the top, otherwise you may never get it off and remain tied to the pontoon for the whole weekend.

There are special cleats that jam the rope just by having the rope wrapped round once. *Jamming cleats* are often used for securing jib and genoa sheets because of the speed with which the line can be jammed on and then freed off.

Back to the task in hand: the sails are up, and we are making progress but the skipper is talking early Greek again.

5
SAILING MANOEUVRES

Well, we came out here to go sailing so that is what we had better do. To make progress we first need to come to terms with the fact that from now on everything we do is determined by the wind, the tide and the *sea state* (whether the sea is rough or not). We have no choice but to work with the elements, unless we put the engine on, and even then we may be limited in what we can do.

As a consequence the position of the boat, the direction it is moving in or towards, and the way the sails are arranged, are described in terms relative to these elements: we can be going towards the wind, to *windward,* or away from it, *downwind*, be going against the tide, *uptide,* or with it, *downtide.* As the boat turns and twists about and as the wind changes direction then these positions change. This is exceedingly confusing to begin with. Our confusion is not helped by the fact that on a boat left is *port* and right is *starboard*, front is *bow*, back is *stern* and in the middle is *beam* or *amidships*. The crucial point to get embedded in the 'little grey cells' is to tune in to the direction of the wind FIRST. Get that clearly established and you are well on the way to understanding the rest.

Being Aware of the Wind

The importance of the wind direction to us is that:
1   We cannot sail directly into the wind, only at an angle towards it, about 45° either side. It is a physical impossibility to sail directly into the wind, no matter how hard we try.
2   The sails have to be let out or pulled in according to the direction we are going relative to the wind, eg going away from the wind we let the sails fully out, going closer to the wind direction, we pull them in tight to get to our 45° angle. The power provided by the wind to drive us along is almost entirely determined by how well we *trim* (adjust) our sails relative to the wind direction. Get it wrong and it is like driving a car with the hand-brake on or in the wrong gear.

It takes time to become sensitive to the direction of the wind, because it is not something we are at all concerned about normally. There may be an electronic instrument on board indicating wind direction, a dial with an arrow pointing which way the boat is going relative to the wind with a red sector, which is the bit we can't sail in; there is likely to be a flag flying at the crosstrees, a *burgee*, and at the stern, the *ensign*; there is usually an instrument like a weather cock on the top of the mast called a wind vane; strips of coloured cloth may be attached to the shrouds called *tell-tales.* All these are a great help, particularly the tell-tales as they are at eye-height; but there is no substitute for getting tuned in yourself to the wind so that it becomes second nature to register that the wind is blowing not just in your face but on to your left cheek, or down your right ear, or on the back of your neck.

Most skippers are very keen to see that the sails are set properly; that any adjustments that have to be made are made quickly; and that when a major course alteration is required the sails are set up correctly for the new wind direction as soon as possible. There is also the problem of *reefing* or reducing sail when the wind strength rises, hoisting more *canvas* (sails) when the wind drops, or becomes light, so that the amount of sail hoisted best matches the wind conditions.

Points of Sailing

First the basic terminology and then the instructions that you are likely to be given by the skipper. Look at the diagram 'Points of Sailing'. You will eventually need to know all the terms given but don't despair, they become second nature once you have been sailing for a few days and we are going to take them in stages. Place the diagram in front of you and imagine you are on a boat and the wind is blowing towards you. If you can arrange a fan to blow directly towards you, this is a great help. Let's start by trying to sail directly into the wind: we can't, so the boat will stop and the sails will flap like mad and the boat is *in stays* or *in irons*. This is not a stable condition; the boat will not just stop, parked waiting for a traffic warden. The wind and tide will eventually cause the boat to *fall away*, either to the left, port or right, starboard.

The boat will not start sailing until the magic 45° angle is made to the wind, and then the boat will only start to move forwards if the sails are pulled in tight. As we are going forward we are on a *tack*; ignore the terms port and starboard for now. We are going as close to the wind direction as we can in order to fill the sails with wind and drive the boat forward (30° would be nice but it doesn't work) and we are *close hauled*: we cannot *haul* the boat any closer to the wind. If we ease out the sails and start to go more sideways, we are then on a *reach* (if you turn sideways to the fan the wind will now be blowing down your ear) and if we turn directly away from the wind we are on a *dead run* or *running before* the wind (turn your back to the fan). Pick all these terms out from the diagram – tack, reach, run.

Remember that the front of the sail is called the luff. Well, look at the diagram and where the boat is going horizontally across the page, sideways to the wind. If we point the front of the boat and therefore the front of the sail more towards the wind, we are *luffing up* to the wind.

Look also at the term reach, again from the sideways position. With the

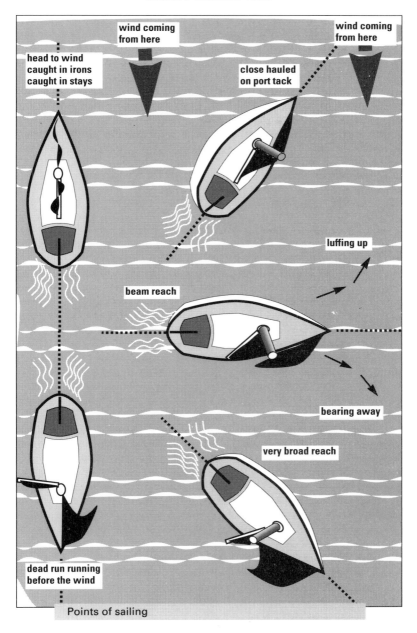

Points of sailing

53

wind coming directly at 90° to the boat over the middle of the boat, the beam, we are said to be on a *beam reach*. If the boat's direction is turned slightly towards the wind, so now the wind is blowing not sideways to the boat but slightly towards it, we are on a *fine* or *close reach*; and if we turn the boat's nose away from the wind so the wind is blowing over our shoulder we are *bearing away* from the wind to go on to a *broad reach*. You will often hear these terms, particularly when being given instructions, such as *luff up* or *bear away*. The skipper might say (if you are lucky), 'I have had enough of bashing away to windward, let's bear away and run off down the coast.'

Tacks and Tacking

Right, leave the diagram for a moment, we will come back to the other terms shown later. On board our skipper has decided he wants to go to windward. We have therefore to pull the sails in tight, both the main and the genoa, and by chance we are heading off with the wind coming into the left side of our face when we look straight down the boat from the cockpit. The boat will be leaning over away from the wind direction, ie to our right, and as the wind is on our left, the port side, we are on a *port tack*.

The skipper decides he wants to *tack*, that is to turn the nose of the boat through the direction of the wind and go off at 45° with the wind coming down the right hand side of the boat. When we have completed this and the wind is coming over the right side of the boat we will then be on a *starboard tack*. We are *tacking*, in fact zig-zagging, towards the wind. To do this we have to co-ordinate our actions with the skipper or *helmsman* (person steering).

The helmsman has to warn us that he is about to turn the ship's wheel or move the tiller and alter course, to give us time to get ready. We have to be ready to let the genoa sheet off, the one that is round the winch and under load and then pull the other *lazy* genoa sheet in once the boat has turned.

The helmsman starts the fun with *Ready About*. This is a question, not a statement. You have to reply either saying yes, or ready, or no, if you are not ready. What you have to do is carefully to ease off the part of the genoa sheet, the one under load, that is tied off round the cleat, but without letting any of the rope slip round the winch. This is very important. If the rope slips and the sail is allowed to flap, there may not be enough momentum to drive the boat's nose round through the wind and we end up stuck half way, in irons.

When we are ready, the helmsman shouts *Lee Oh* and moves the wheel or tiller. The nose of the boat starts to point towards the wind and as soon as the genoa starts to flap you pull off all the turns of rope round the winch and check that the rope runs freely through the block in front and doesn't jam.

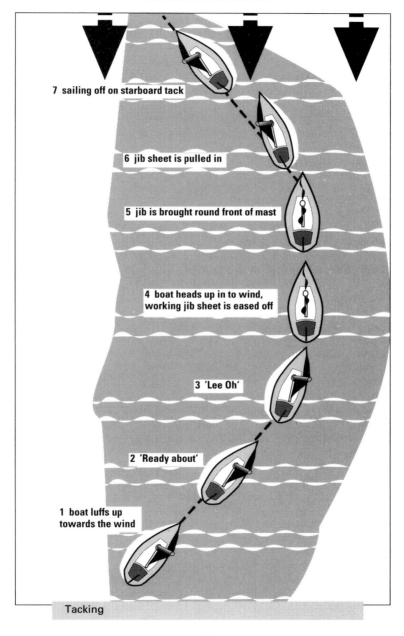

7 sailing off on starboard tack

6 jib sheet is pulled in

5 jib is brought round front of mast

4 boat heads up in to wind, working jib sheet is eased off

3 'Lee Oh'

2 'Ready about'

1 boat luffs up towards the wind

Tacking

The crew on the other side of the cockpit now pull in their loose genoa sheet as fast as they can, having taken just one turn round their winch. The next stage is also critical as timing is of the essence. Once most of the loose sheet has been pulled in and BEFORE the wind fills the genoa again at least two more turns of the rope are taken round the winch, then the winch handle is put in the top of the winch and the sheet is pulled in as tight as the skipper wants. If the wind gets into the genoa before the extra turns are on, the only safe thing to do is to ease out the genoa sheet until the sail flaps, then get the extra turns on round the winch and start grinding away, only now you have a lot more rope to pull in and it is under load.

Note than no one has had to touch the main sheet. The boom just flops over from one side of the boat to the other, and the main sheet itself is not touched.

Running Before the Wind

Fortunately the skipper has had enough of going to windward and decides he wants to run off before the wind. He wants to alter course and says *Bearing Away*. This may be followed with the instruction *Ease Sheets*; whether given or not, that is what you have to do. The boat's nose is turned away from the direction of the wind and keeps turning until the wind goes round towards the back of the boat. Note that the wind has not changed direction, you have changed your direction relative to the wind. As the wind will now blow from the back of the boat towards the front, we have to let out the main sheet and the genoa sheet. As you ease out the main sheet, the boom swings towards the mast; it can only go so far and then it hits the shrouds. Most skippers like the boom kept just off the shrouds and not pressing against them. The genoa needs to be eased out until it begins to flap and then be brought back in a little. WE ARE NOW ON THE MOST DANGEROUS POINT OF SAILING. Why?

Just a slight mistake by the helmsman or a slight change in the wind direction and there could be an *all standing gybe*. What happens is that the wind pushes the main and therefore the boom rapidly from one side of the boat to the other. This is a major cause of accidents on boats because being hit on the head by the boom or even by the main sheet as the boom whips from one side to the other nearly always causes an injury, sometimes, it has to be said, a fatal injury. It does not do the boat much good either and can damage the boom, boom end fittings, even bring the mast down. A prudent skipper, especially one constantly reminded by the crew, needs to *rig* (fit) a rope, called a *preventer* or more fully a *boom guy preventer*, running from the end of the boom to a block on the foredeck and then back to the cockpit (so that it can be adjusted or let go if necessary), to stop this happening. If we want to alter course when running down wind, then we *gybe* the main under control.

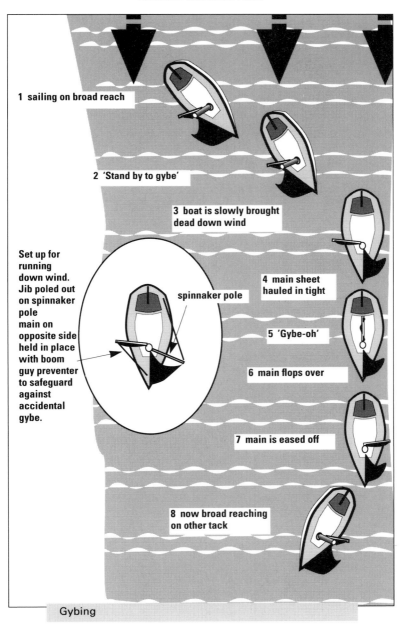

1 sailing on broad reach

2 'Stand by to gybe'

3 boat is slowly brought dead down wind

Set up for running down wind. Jib poled out on spinnaker pole main on opposite side held in place with boom guy preventer to safeguard against accidental gybe.

spinnaker pole

4 main sheet hauled in tight

5 'Gybe-oh'

6 main flops over

7 main is eased off

8 now broad reaching on other tack

Gybing

57

Gybing

This time the helmsman starts by saying *Stand by to gybe*. THIS IS NOT AN INVITATION TO STAND UP! Either the helmsman or a crewmember will grab the main sheet, and as the helmsman gradually alters course, so that the wind instead of say coming over his left shoulder starts to blow down his neck, any slack in the main sheet is hauled in. By the time the wind is directly astern the main sheet should be tight in with the boom more or less pointing straight down the middle of the boat. As the helmsman continues slowly to alter course, the wind comes the other side of the sail, this flips the boom over, but now it has to travel only a few inches; and once the boom has flopped over from one side to the other, with the wind now blowing over the helmsman's right shoulder, the main sheet is very quickly eased out again.

The genoa also has to be taken over from one side to the other using the sheets and winches but the critical move is the one with the main. The key to the gybing manoeuvre is again co-ordination, as well as the helmsman taking his time in altering course. If a preventer was *rigged* before the gybe, then this has to be removed or eased off before starting the manoeuvre, and then set up again on the other side. Above all, remember gybing under control is safe, out of control is lethal, and you never stand up in the cockpit when going dead downwind.

Well, we can tack and gybe, what else is there to prevent us getting bored or remembering we feel sea-sick? The skipper decides he wants to run downwind *wing and wing*, or *goose winging*. Sounds intriguing. If you look at the 'points of sailing' diagram again, at the bottom you will see a picture of a boat with the main sail out one side of the boat and the genoa out the other. That is what we are being asked to do. Assuming our main has been re-rigged with a preventer after our gybe, then it is going to stay put and we have to pull the genoa round to the other side of the boat by easing off the working sheet and pulling in on the lazy sheet.

Poling out the Genoa

The helmsman needs to get the angle of the wind coming down the boat exactly right in order to keep both the main and the genoa filled with wind. If there are any waves around this becomes difficult. As the boat rolls from one side to the other (as it tends to do when sailing down wind) the wind is *spilled,* the power of the wind is lost, and the genoa keeps collapsing. To stop this the skipper asks us to *pole it out*. We are certainly having a busy first day at sea. Remember on our tour of the boat we came across a long metal tube lashed to the deck, called a spinnaker pole, well this is the pole being referred to. It has to be taken off the deck, attached at one end to the mast, held out at right angles to the boat (with ropes, don't panic) and the genoa sheet led through the end. Sounds horrendous but once again after you have done this a few times it ceases to be a problem, the difficulty is more one of balancing yourself while the boat rolls.

Look first at the diagram to see what we are trying to achieve. We need to use three new ropes, each with their own names, a *downhaul*, an *uphaul* and a guy or *after guy*. The uphaul will already be fitted to the mast. This is a thinnish line, with a snapshackle on one end. The line does not go to the top of the mast like a halliard but about halfway up and then comes down again. The skipper will give you the downhaul, another lightish line with a snapshackle on the end, and the guy which is likely to be thicker and be used for many purposes. It also has a snapshackle on the end of it.

Before the spinnaker pole is taken off the deck the downhaul is clipped onto a U-shaped fitting somewhere towards the end of the

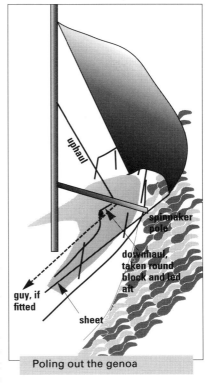

uphaul

spinnaker pole

downhaul, taken round block and led aft

guy, if fitted

sheet

Poling out the genoa

pole and the other end made fast on the foredeck, but you must leave plenty of slack to enable you to move the pole. The pole is now unlashed and one end clipped into a fitting that runs along a track up and down the front of the mast; the other end is pointed towards the front of the boat and rested on the deck. We clip on the uphaul to the top of the pole. We attach the after guy to the pole and rig so that it goes to the very back of the boat. Now comes the tricky bit. What we want to do is hoist the pole (hence the term uphaul) so that it sticks out sideways and doesn't bounce about all over the place. The three lines you have rigged control this perfectly because they all pull against each other.

You hoist the pole with the uphaul to the right height (the skipper will advise, but it should be at right angles to the mast and point out at the same height as the clew of the genoa) and cleat off the uphaul on a small cleat on the side of the mast. You grab hold of the downhaul and pull on this to stop the pole lifting up any further (hence the term downhaul) and as the crew in

59

the cockpit pull on the after guy, pulling the pole outwards over the side of the boat, you gently ease out the downhaul. When the pole is in the correct position, the downhaul is cleated off on the foredeck, or it may be taken back through blocks to the cockpit. The after guy is also cleated off.

So we have got the pole out and held in place by the three lines, the uphaul, downhaul and guy, but how does this help hold the sail out? Well it doesn't, unless the genoa sheet also runs through the outside end of the pole. At the end of the pole is a fitting that looks like a piston hank. You pull on the piston part, the jaws open and the sheet drops in. It clearly is a physical impossibility to do this once the pole is in position poking out over the side of the boat, unless you have ten foot long arms. The line must be fed through before the pole is pulled out. The easy way to do this is to start with the genoa on the opposite side to where it is to be poled out. Then all you have to do is to take the lazy genoa sheet which is not under any load and clip it through the end of the pole. Once the pole is in position the helmsman can alter course and the sail is simply pulled round from one side of the boat to the other as normal, except the sheet is now running through the end of the pole and the pole is keeping the sail fully open.

Unfortunately for us as foredeck crew, what is more often the case is that the skipper, safe in the cockpit, decides to put the pole up with the genoa already flying on the side he wants it poled out; and rather than make life easier and alter course for a few minutes and pull the genoa round to the other side decides we can cope 'if we are quick'. The way this works is that when the pole is ready to be pulled out the genoa sheet under load is let loose and the genoa flaps like mad. We have to grab the sheet that is flying all over the place and put it through the end of the pole. Once that is done the sheet and guy are hauled back in and we look after the downhaul.

Another common variation is not to use an after guy. In this case the pole is pulled back and out, by pulling in on the genoa sheet so that the clew pulls the pole out. It works, but the pole is not under the same control. If the pole is held in place with three separate lines, then if we need to alter course quickly, we can; and the pole stays in place even if the genoa is pulled round to the other side. Without the guy, the pole swings forward as soon as the genoa sheet is let off.

Another variation sometimes seen is to attach the pole directly to the clew of the sail. If you are asked to do this, find a new skipper.

6
REEFING

After a while, just when we were beginning to relax and enjoy ourselves, our skipper decides the wind is *piping up* and it looks as though it might blow a *hooley* (strongly; I think the term comes from hooligan). A good skipper is one that reefs early, though you may not always agree if it means prancing around the foredeck changing headsails.

At the moment we are sailing downwind, wing and wing, with the spinnaker pole out, so first we have to take down our spinnaker pole, remove and stow the lines and secure the pole to the deck. The pole usually fits in to a metal cradle located on the side deck or on the coachroof, although sometimes it is stored vertically against the mast. Next comes the genoa itself.

Reefing the Genoa

With sails that are hanked on with piston hanks, the whole sail has to come down and be changed for a smaller one. This takes time and is not easy if the boat is bouncing. The whole sequence that we went through in harbour has to be reversed. The genoa halliard has to be let off, under control, and the sail dropped down onto the foredeck, gathered up and tied off to the rails with sail ties. The halliard has to be carefully unclipped from the head of the sail and then clipped securely somewhere close by, onto the pulpit or the base of a stanchion post. The bowlines attaching the sheets to the sail have to be untied and the loose ends made fast to a safety rail or stanchion post. The sail has to be put into the sail bag, and now is when you are likely to lose the bag if it is not tied on. The clew is pushed to the bottom of the bag.

Next, starting at the head, each of the piston hanks is unclipped and then the sail is progressively stuffed into the bag. The last bit to go in should be the tack as this is the first bit you will need when you want to put the sail up again. The sail bag is dragged back to the cockpit and the next sail taken forward in its bag. Tie the bag on. Hank the sail on, starting at the tack, fitting each piston hank on in turn making sure the luff is not twisted; drag the sail down the side deck, put on sail ties, and tie the sheets on with bowlines. Finally the halliard is attached and the sail is ready to be

61

hoisted under control. This is a long and very sick making job in any sort of sea and all the time the headsail is down the boat cannot be sailed very efficiently.

If as crew we are clear what is required and the boat has been set up correctly, we can cut down the time the boat does not have a head sail set by getting the next sail ready to hoist before dropping the one that is up. We do this by taking the next sail up to the foredeck, clipping on the tack to a second shackle previously fitted for the purpose, then clipping on each piston hank on the forestay between the tack of the other sail and its first piston hank. If there is not enough space then we have to undo the first piston hank on the sail that is up, which may not be easy. The sail that is up is then dropped, sheets transferred, piston hanks taken off, stuffed in its bag, the halliard transferred and the new sail hoisted.

It takes no imagination to see that most crew would be grateful for improvements to this system. The usual scenario is that the wind has come up during the night, it has started raining, the seas are building and the skipper has held on far too long with too much sail up hoping things would get better. Now the headsail has to be changed. I have lost count of the number of times I have been bounced off my backside onto a cleat, whilst sitting on the foredeck, fighting with sailcloth and pistons that won't come undone, with wellingtons completely full of water. It's not nice.

Luff grooves The first partial improvement was the invention of luff grooves or tubes that run up the whole of the forestay. You may well come across this. Instead of having to fit piston hanks, all that is required is to feed the luff of the sail, which has a rope sewn all down the front edge to make a bulge, into a grooved sleeve around the forestay (see diagram page 49). Usually there is a device called a self-feeder which means, once you have got the sail started in the groove, simply pulling on the halliard feeds the rest of the sail into the groove. Very quick and no broken finger nails. And if you can have one groove, you can have two, and so the second sail can be ready to hoist as the first is dropped. Two halliards and two sets of sheets and you can put one sail up on the inside of the other and then drop the outside one. There are two disadvantages: one, you are still on the foredeck getting wet; two, when the sail is dropped it comes out of the groove and flies all over the foredeck unless you keep it under control. Unlike the sail with hanks, it is no longer attached to the forestay, just to the halliard.

Roller furling headsails The biggest improvement as far as crew are concerned has been the introduction of roller furling headsails. These sails do not set quite so well, therefore they don't create the same power but they are a delight to use as everything is controlled from the cockpit. No more filled wellies! The sail is hoisted in exactly the same way as with the foil system, sheets attached. The sail slides up a grooved tube that runs the length of the forestay. At the bottom near the deck there is a drum attached to the tube, and wound round the drum is wire, or more commonly thin rope, that leads through blocks all the way back to the cockpit. The system works like a roller blind. To wind the sail around the tube which freely rotates around the forestay, you pull on the line. This spins the drum round and winds in the sail cloth. To pull out the sail you ease off the line and pull hard on the sheets. Thus if you want to reduce sail area you just pull on the furling line in the cockpit and the sail gets smaller as it is rolled in round the forestay. No sheets to change, no going on foredeck, no halliard to change over. Want to increase the sail area? Then you just ease off on the furling line and pull hard on the sheets. Good news for crew! The sail is often left up all season, just rolled away when the boat comes in to harbour.

Reefing the Main

What about the main? Well, there have been lots of attempts to produce similar roller systems with varying degrees of success. Apart from some fairly unusual and expensive systems around, you are most likely to be faced with a variant of the same method that has been used for years, called *slab* or *jiffy* reefing. The biggest advances made in this system have come about with improvements to ropes and pulleys together with new rope jammers, also called locks or *clutches*. Look at the diagram on page 64 and the principle is obvious. All that is happening is that a section at the bottom of the main is being taken out of service. This has two advantages: first the actual area of sail cloth is reduced, which reduces the amount of power the sail can produce, and second, the height of the sail is reduced, which also helps reduce power, as wind speed increases dramatically with height, especially in the first ten metres or so. We are into new ropes and new terms again but most importantly try and understand what is happening rather than worrying about all the names.

Look at the luff of the main and you will see that at set stages going up the sail there are things called *reefing cringles*. These are metal rings or hoops set into the sail, with the surrounding sailcloth heavily strengthened. Where the boom joins the mast are at least two round-ended metal hooks, one each side of the boom. All we have to do is lower the main halliard far enough for the ring or cringle to go over a hook, and tighten up the halliard again, it is as simple as that.

We need to reduce the sail along the whole length of the foot and so we need to take in a similar amount of sail at the back or leech of the sail. We also need to be able to pull the foot back, in the same way that the clew outhaul works on the full size main. This is very important as it reduces the curve in the sail and a flatter sail has less power. The last thing we want if we are reefing to reduce power, is to have a main with a great bag of a

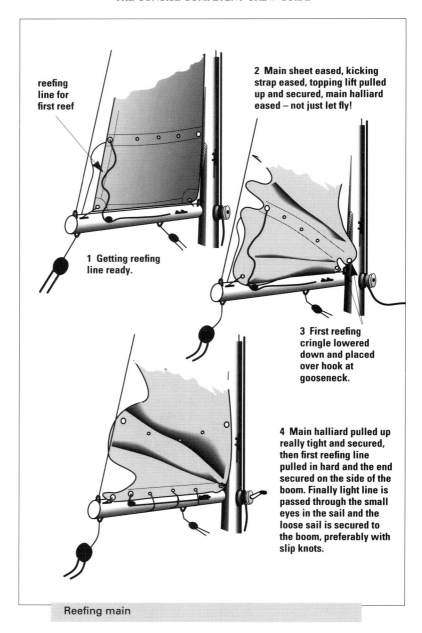

reefing
line for
first reef

1 Getting reefing
line ready.

2 Main sheet eased, kicking
strap eased, topping lift pulled
up and secured, main halliard
eased – not just let fly!

3 First reefing
cringle lowered
down and placed
over hook at
gooseneck.

4 Main halliard pulled up
really tight and secured,
then first reefing line
pulled in hard and the end
secured on the side of the
boom. Finally light line is
passed through the small
eyes in the sail and the
loose sail is secured to
the boom, preferably with
slip knots.

Reefing main

64

curve in it. Not only does this increase power it makes the boat more diffi-cult to steer and makes it *heel* (tip over) much more.

Reefing lines So we can't simply hook the back of the sail down. A rope is tied to a fitting at the back of the boom, is led up the back of the sail through another cringle, back down to the boom again, round a block and then is taken forward. Pull hard on this line and you not only reduce the amount of sail, you pull the reefing cringle out towards the end of the boom and flatten the sail. Again, very simple. The rope is called a *reefing line*; it is usual for the main to have three reefing points, and the ropes follow the sequence of first reefing line, second reefing line etc. It is normal to have the lines for the first two reefs rigged available for use at all times, but some-times the third reef is not rigged until the weather forecast looks as though it might be needed (in which case it is time to head for harbour fast).

The reefing lines may run down the outside of the boom and have their own small winch and cleats on the side of the boom; they may run down the inside and come out nearer the mast; they may come out under the boom through a series of jammers and be led to a winch fixed to the mast under the gooseneck; or they may be taken all the way back to the cockpit. Depending on how the system is set up, the whole operation of reefing the main can be carried out at the mast or in the cockpit. Although it is much safer working at the mast than on the foredeck, it is safer still in the cockpit.

How to do it Our skipper wants the first reef put in and everything is at the mast. The sequence is as follows:

1 One or two crew to mast, going down opposite side-deck to where boom is (the crew are going down the *windward* side of the boat)

2 The main sheet is eased in the cockpit to provide some slack

3 At the mast, first the kicker under the boom is eased and then the end of the boom is pulled up a little on the *topping lift* (without the topping lift on, the boom would drop onto your fellow crewmembers in the cockpit)

4 The main halliard is eased slowly while the luff of the sail is pulled down to the first reefing cringle and the cringle is put over the hook

5 The halliard is now pulled up tight again, using a winch, and cleated off

6 The first reefing line is found and pulled in hard, pulling the leech of the sail down. It is important to make sure there is enough slack in the main and kicker to enable the reefing cringle at the back of the sail to come all the way down to join the boom. Winch in the reefing line to the skipper's require-ments, not so hard that you rip the sail, and cleat off

7 Ease off the topping lift

8 Pull in on the kicker

9 Tidy all lines and then return to the cockpit, again on the safe (uphill) side, opposite the boom.

Once this is practised it can be done very quickly, with no instructions, even at night. It is noisy because the sail is flapping and the noise can make the situation seem dramatic at times, but it is an easy, quick and efficient way of reducing sail.

After the mainsail has been reefed There is still some tidying up to do. The skipper may want the *bunt* or bag of spare sail that is now hanging under the boom to be lashed to the boom using short *reefing pennants* or lines. These are a pain if they are not permanently fixed as otherwise you have to thread thin bits of string through tiny metal rings in the sail while balancing on the coachroof, hanging on to the boom and hoping the helmsman is concentrating and does not alter course until you have finished and are safely back in the cockpit. The second reefing line will now be very loose and hang under the boom and the slack needs to be taken out of this line by pulling on the end, wherever that may be, at the mast or in the cockpit.

The improvement to conditions on board by reefing has to be experienced to be fully appreciated. One minute the boat is heeling right over and is obviously not under proper control, being very difficult to steer; reef the sails and the heeling decreases, the boat can be steered and it is time for congratulations all round and a cup of tea. If the wind drops then it is equally easy to shake out the reef. Ease the main sheet, ease the kicker, pull in the topping lift, free off the reefing line, ease the halliard enough to get the cringle off the hook at the front of the boom, hoist the main, ease off the topping lift, pull in on the main, pull in on the kicker, tidy all lines.

Our skipper is well pleased with his able crew and has had a great day sailing; but enough is enough, and he has decided to look for a sheltered anchorage for the night and asks us to get the anchor out of its locker and stow it on the bow roller, and to *flake out*, or lay out, the chain on the side deck.

Is the crew's work never done?

7

ANCHORS AND ANCHORING

The three activities guaranteed to fray the nerves of even the most easy-going skipper are dropping the anchor, attaching the boat to a mooring buoy, and messing about in marinas. In terms of creating tension on board, the last of the three is without doubt the best. Anchoring does have its moments however, and as you most certainly will be blamed for whatever goes wrong, it pays to have some idea of what is expected of you – usually the impossible. It helps to know what the skipper is trying to achieve, which may not be all that easy to discern, either from what the boat is doing or from the often confused and confusing instructions coming your way.

Starting as always with the basics, we will look at the most common types of anchor and how they work. Next comes how to use them and what is expected of you as crew; and finally the odd difficult situation you might come across, other than a belligerent skipper who blames you when the anchor doesn't work. There are a just a few new words and phrases to learn this time, not like the previous section.

How Anchors Work

There is an understandable notion that an anchor works at holding a boat in place by being very heavy. Drop a heavy lump of metal on the sea-bed with a line attached to it and you will stay put. This is unfortunately not the case. The anchors you see on big merchant vessels tend to operate in this way, but not those found on yachts. For an anchor to be effective simply by weight alone, it has to be big and heavy. Carting a heavy weight around on a yacht is going to do nothing for the boat's speed. Also, anchors tend to be kept either at the very front or near the front of boats and so the weight of an anchor and its chain will affect the boat's balance and make the nose tip downwards. The heavier the anchor the more this will upset the balance.

Finally and not the least reason, unlike merchant ships, small boats are not normally blessed with huge hydraulic winches available to raise and lower the anchor at the press of a button. On most yachts the anchor will be handled by you, the crew. If you are lucky there may be a special winch to help, sometimes called simply an anchor winch, sometimes a *windlass*.Very occasionally there may be a powered winch, but normally it is down to you; and even with a manual windlass it can still seem like hard work.

Well, if it is not simply weight, how does the anchor work? The idea is that it should grab hold of the sea-bed and hook the boat on securely (you may hear the phrase *dropping the hook*). The differing designs go about this task in slightly different ways but they all have the same primary objective of providing a secure attachment to the sea-bed, capable of withstanding the substantial pull exerted when a boat is at anchor in strong currents or winds. The second objective, and here is the catch, is that the anchor must be capable of being easily unstuck or raised when it is time to move off to harbours new.

Another problem anchors have to contend with is the state of the sea-bed. On the surface all we have is wind, water and skippers, all in varying degrees of agitation – the sea-bed can be hard rock to soft mud. It can also be completely bare or covered in anything from tin cans to seaweed ten feet thick. Now perhaps you can begin to understand why the skipper looks less than relaxed. He does have some information to guide him however, as the charts show the general make up of the sea-bed.

Where to Anchor

If you look carefully at a chart you will see amongst all the other seemingly meaningless abbreviations one- and two-letter codes over the sea areas saying what the sea-bed is like, eg S for sand, M for mud, Sn for shingle. The lettering is quite small but it is there. The skipper also has information on the chart about good and bad anchorages. A symbol of an anchor is often used to indicate a good spot and there may be additional information in small type to help him find the correct location. If the sea-bed is known to have problems the term *foul* may be seen.

He also has information in the other publications called *Almanacs* and local *Pilots*; these often have simple drawings or chart extracts in them indicating safe anchorages. We will look at these in more detail later. As everyone tends to have the same information, the most well known anchorages can become very crowded places, which adds to the skipper's problems when selecting his spot; this is nothing like parking a car in a marked space.

Types of Anchor

We have yet to examine the contents of our anchor locker but the anchor is likely to be one of five main types, each with their own characteristics; you need to know them, their good and bad points and how to use them safely. There are variations on these same themes around, as well as anchors designed to meet local conditions and anchors for use in dinghies. Anchor technology is alive and well and new designs are coming out all the time,

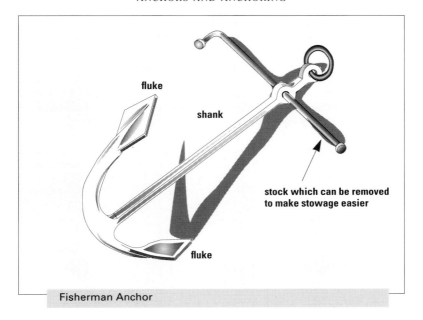

Fisherman Anchor

with great claims being made for them; but once you recognise the five main types, you can usually place any new ones in one of these groups.

The Fisherman The title is a bit misleading as the anchor is not confined to use on fishing boats; another term that might be used is *traditional*. This is the anchor we all think of as being an anchor: it is the symbol used outside pubs, on clothes, in books. It is not commonly found on the decks of a modern yacht but you may find a small version lurking at the bottom of a cockpit locker. If you go flotilla cruising in the Mediterranean you may well find one tied to the rails at the back of your boat, with its chain stowed in a bucket underneath for reasons which we will examine later.

A Fisherman Anchor (see diagram above) is made up of two main parts, the *shank,* which divides in two, with hooks or *flukes* on each end, and a bar or *stock*, which goes at right angles to the flukes. The most important thing is to understand how it works. When the anchor is lowered to the sea-bed, the bar ensures that one or other of the flukes makes contact with the bottom. It should be impossible for the anchor to come to rest with the two flukes lying flat on the sea-bed. Pulling on the line attached to the anchor should cause one of the flukes to stick in the sea-bed.

Advantages: The Fisherman is excellent on rocky or weed-covered sea-beds. The flukes usually penetrate weed well, as they are relatively narrow

THE CONCISE COMPETENT CREW GUIDE

and sharp. The design has stood the test of time and you will still see fisherman anchors around, particularly on larger craft. It is still used on lifeboats and is a good emergency anchor to have on board a yacht, as it may work when all others have failed.

Disadvantages: For the anchor to work well, it needs to be of a substantial size and therefore weight. Added to this disadvantage for yachts and powerboats, it is large and awkward to use, and difficult to stow on deck ready for immediate use. To aid stowage problems the bar or stock may be removable, but obviously has to be pinned back in place before the anchor can be used again. It is not good at holding in soft sea-bed conditions, such as mud, loose sand, shingle etc. It is easy to make a mistake when actually using it and to get the anchor line wrapped round the fluke that sticks up from the sea-bed.

There is no doubt however that it is an effective anchor when used properly; it really comes in to its own on larger boats where it can be held in place over the side, ready for immediate use.

Plough or CQR Anchor Generally regarded by most as the best anchor invented to date; you will certainly come across this one when crewing on modern yachts and powerboats. Its seeming simplicity, a wobbly plough shape on the end of a long stick, belies the sophistication of the design and relatively recent origins – it was designed for use on flying boats. Professor Sir Geoffrey Taylor produced the design in the UK in 1933, after prolonged research into the design of an anchor that would hold a flying boat, with the substantial drag caused by the plane's windage, in all types of locations, and yet still be light enough to be carried on board.

The way it grabs the sea-bed, as you might expect from the name and shape, is by ploughing itself into the ground. The subtlety of the design is contained in the precise angles of the blades and the relationship of their size to that of the long shaft, the joint between the shaft and the end, and the bend in the shaft itself. The anchor will not work if these are wrong.

The anchor does not pull into the sea-bed quite as you might imagine. It is designed so that it will pull in on its side, not both plough shares at the same time, although the skipper hopes they will both end up being buried. It does need to be pulled more or less horizontally along the sea-bed to work, a common feature with most small-boat anchors.

Advantages: The CQR has been tested repeatedly and found to have excellent holding characteristics, especially where it can bury itself into secure ground. It has a good power to weight ratio, that is to say it does not need to be so heavy to have the same effect as say a fisherman anchor. It is easy to lay and usually easy to retrieve as the long shaft provides a lot of leverage to help pull the anchor free. The pivot joint enables a certain amount of movement of the yacht around the anchor should the wind

70

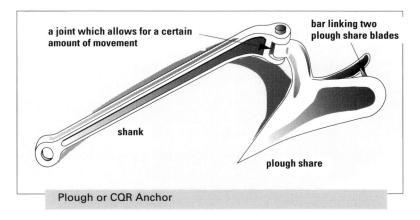

a joint which allows for a certain
amount of movement

bar linking two
plough share blades

shank

plough share

Plough or CQR Anchor

change direction or the tide turn and try to drag the yacht off to pastures new. Even if the anchor is pulled free from its original position and *breaks out*, it usually quickly ploughs itself back in again – a very useful feature at 3am because as crew you will have the job of groping your way up to the foredeck in the wind and the rain (it always rains when the anchor drags), if the anchor doesn't *bite* (grip) and needs to be properly laid again.

Where the sea-bed is known to have obstructions on it, or where there are a lot of other boats nearby with their anchor lines forming an underwater cats-cradle, it is easy to attach another lighter line to the anchor, either to the bar between the two plough shares, or through a specially provided hole, to give a second angle of pull should the anchor get fouled-up. This line is called a *tripping line*, for the obvious reason that it 'trips up' the anchor.

Disadvantages: It is still a big chunk of metal to grab hold of, and the long shaft adds leverage. It is ideal as far as safehandling is concerned if the anchor is permanently stowed, ready for use, over the bow rollers, but then it adds weight in exactly the wrong place and as a consequence it is normally tied down on deck or put inside the anchor locker. The crew have the unenviable task of picking the anchor up and threading the awkward plough-shaped end past an obstacle course of bits of wire, metal rails etc, in order to rest it over the front of the boat. It does not hold well on rock, unless it jams in a crevice, or where the bottom is covered in thick weed. If the ground is very soft mud, or perhaps shingle, it has the disconcerting habit of digging in enough to fool you and then ploughing gently along, a few feet at a time, while you, unawares, sleep off your lunch in the cockpit.

I have been given two explanations for the term CQR: one is Coastal Quick Release, not the right one I think, and the other – say CQR over and over quickly and you will soon get the idea.

The Bruce Anchor The Bruce Anchor is yet another anchor designed to serve a particular purpose as far removed from small boat sailing as possible, and yet very popular now on yachts and commercial vessels worldwide. The anchor was designed by Peter Bruce in 1972 for use in securing oil rigs in the North Sea. The design requirement was to produce an anchor that could hold static loads on short anchor lines; for short read anchor lines that make a steep angle with the sea-bed, as opposed to say the CQR which works best when the pull is horizontally along the sea-bed.

Like the CQR it is a self-burying anchor, and again the sophistication of the design is not immediately apparent. When it hits the bottom, one fluke is always ready to dig in. A strong pull on the anchor line should see all three large flukes buried with the shank sticking upwards out of the sea-bed.

Advantages The claims made for this anchor are that it has a good power to weight ratio, so that the anchor does not have to be so heavy; and that once dug in, it has high holding power. There are no moving parts to get jammed or fouled, and as it is designed to work on a shorter *scope* (length) of chain, it is useful in a crowded anchorage as the boat does not require so much room to *swing* (I will explain what this means shortly) and it is easy to clean.

Disadvantages It is not very good where the bottom is foul with weeds, as the large flukes cannot cut through; similarly it is not very good on hard ground. It can be difficult to bury properly, and once buried is difficult to

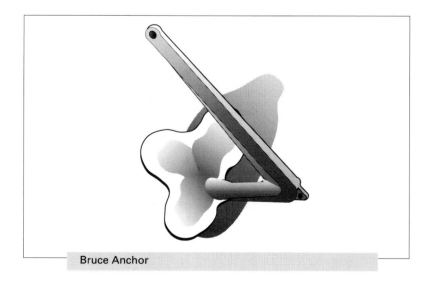

Bruce Anchor

retrieve. It may well be heavier coming up than going down as the whole of the bowl shape formed by the flukes can be full of mud. It is not thought to be so good at holding, when the tide turns and pulls the boat and hence the anchor chain in a different direction, and once broken out may not re-lay itself. It is not easy to stow on deck and requires a largish anchor locker. It has the same problem as the plough anchor of being an awkward shape to feed through the pulpit past the forestay, but with a shorter shank and lighter weight is easier to handle than the plough. It is a highly popular anchor on yachts, both as a *bower* (main) anchor and as a *kedge* (sec-ondary) anchor.

The Danforth This term covers a whole group of anchors and their history goes back a long way. The name Danforth comes from R. Danforth, an American, who in 1939, developed the basic pattern for the modern type of Danforth. What is not apparent from the diagram is that the shank is pivoted about the stock at the crown. At rest the anchor stows flat. Pick up the shank and the two flukes drop down to a set angle. The way it works is that the anchor is weighted at the crown such that the crown and stock hit the bottom first. As the anchor is pulled across the sea-bed, the arms of the stock stop the anchor twisting, keeping it level while the flukes bury them-selves into the sea-bed. As the flukes are quite large, once buried they provide a very strong grip. There are lots of variations of this type, some without stocks, some with smaller flukes, or different shaped flukes and they go under such names as the Fob and the Brittany.

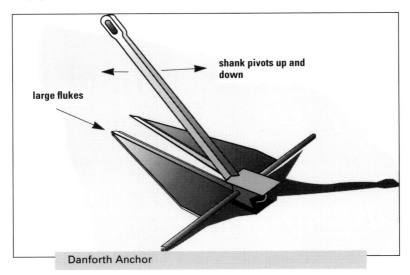

large flukes

shank pivots up and down

Danforth Anchor

73

Advantages Of all the anchors they are the easiest to stow on deck as they stow flat; the only projection to catch rope is the crown. They have a reasonable power to weight ratio but size does help. They are good at burying in the right sea-bed conditions; not in rock or hard ground, but may be marginally better than say a Bruce at penetrating light weed. The various angles involved are not so critical as the Plough and the Bruce and the anchor is therefore easier to make, but the components must still be exceptionally strong.

Disadvantages They can be very difficult to get up again, so much so that they can be damaged. The shank may get bent, or the flukes, and if severely distorted, the anchor looses efficiency. The joint must be kept free of barnacles and similar growths or else the anchor does not work at all. They are not particularly good at relaying themselves; if the anchor breaks out when the tide turns, it can skate across the sea-bed and have to be hauled up and carefully relaid again.

The Folding Grapnel Not in the big league and certainly not to be used as the main anchor, but the Folding Grapnel Anchor can usually be found lurking in the bottom of the cockpit locker. The design is a bit like an upside down umbrella. The flukes are held in place against the shank by a ring. Turn the ring and the flukes drop down. It is used mainly as a dinghy anchor as it stows away so easily and the flukes are out of harm's way, particularly useful in a rubber dinghy. It has very little holding power but it makes you feel like a proper sailor to have one in the dinghy. It has a major, non direct anchoring use, and that is as a hook to help lift your proper anchor chain if there is a problem on the sea-bed.

Anchor Cable

How well the anchor works depends not just on the design of the anchor but how it is attached to the boat, whether by chain or by a mixture of chain and rope. There is much more to the design of chain than is apparent, and it has a long history, going back to the early 1800s. It is sufficient for us to know why it is used; it is not simply its inherent strength.

Weight Most anchors require as nearly a horizontal pull across the sea bed as possible to dig in. The weight of the chain, assuming enough is let out at the right time, ensures that as the boat travels away from the anchor, the correct angle is achieved.

Resistance to damage The anchor must withstand constant abrasion against the sea-bed and against rocks, and lengthy immersion in salt water and even withstand being hit by another boat's hull or propeller. It is stowed away wet.

Shock absorbing qualities If a boat was connected almost directly in a straight line with the sea-bed by a taut anchor cable, with every wave that hit the hull and gust of the wind, the boat would jerk, risking damaging the boat or pulling out the anchor. The weight of the chain makes it form a gentle curve between the anchor and the boat, and so when a shock load hits the boat, the boat drifts gently back as the cable rises slightly to absorb the increased load. When the load is reduced, the weight of the cable brings the boat gently forward again.

Anchor Rope

With so much going for it, why is chain ever mixed with rope? Chain is very heavy. It adds to the problem that already exists of having the heavy weight of the anchor at the bow affecting the balance of the boat. Add the weight of the chain to the anchor and then anchor in more than 10 metres (33ft) of water, and the crew have got a lot of weight to retrieve from the sea-bed, hence the need for windlasses. As a compromise on some boats, particularly racing boats, the anchor *rode* is made up of a length of chain and then rope. The longer the length of chain before any rope is joined on, the better the anchor will work and the quieter the boat will lie at an anchorage. As there is little weight in the rope, much more has to be paid out to get anything like the same holding power. Nylon rope does stretch under load and thereby help to act as a shock absorber, but there is no substitute for an all-chain anchor cable.

Laying an Anchor

Our skipper has recently purchased a bigger (and heavier) Plough which he has secured to the chain and managed to jam in the foredeck locker. First we open the anchor locker and secure the lid with a piece of *shock cord* (elastic rope) that is permanently attached, to prevent the heavy fibreglass lid from dropping back down on our wrists. The anchor is on top of all the chain and secured in place with light lines to prevent it moving around in the locker and damaging the boat. The anchor has to be carefully extracted, taken forward, placed over the bow roller and secured.

It is common, as in our case, for the bow roller to have a pin through the side, just like one of the shackles, and this pin goes through the shank of the anchor and locks into place on the other side of the bow roller. Watch your fingers as the anchor is very heavy and if the boat is rolling or going up and down the shank will trap your fingers. Also watch your back and when you lift the anchor forward, do so with a straight back and bent legs, not the other way round.

But before even attempting any of this, we pull some chain out of the locker and secure the chain around a cleat, just enough *scope* (length) to enable us to take the anchor forward to the bow roller. In a cartoon it would be funny if someone accidentally dropped the anchor overboard and the boat was *brought up short, all standing*. In real life it is not, especially as the natural reaction of anyone is to try and redeem the situation and grab or stamp on the chain as it flies out of the locker. If the anchor goes, leap out of the way. There is no alternative. Only once all the anchor chain has gone and you are down to the *bitter end* (a piece of light line that is tied onto the anchor chain and secured in the bottom of the locker; it comes out onto the deck to enable you either to add rope to the chain or, in an emergency, to cut the anchor free) can you and the skipper start to get the situation back under control.

We have been asked to flake out the chain. All this means is drag the chain out of the locker and lay it up and down the side deck.

The chain should have some sort of marks along its length indicating distance from the anchor, in metres, feet or fathoms (rare). The marks often wear off or the skipper may have forgotten what system he used last year, was one stripe 10 metres and two stripes 20 metres, or was the first stripe at 30 feet? It is usual to be asked to flake out the chain in approximately equal lengths of about 10 feet or 2 metres and to be able to tell the skipper how much chain you have on the side deck. You are not expected to get all the chain out of the locker. Now comes the interesting bit.

The skipper will tell you approximately how deep the water will be where he intends anchoring so you can work out how much of the chain on the deck this is equivalent to. We are anchoring with the sails still up. The skipper gently turns the boat up into the wind, the boat slows down and gradually stops making progress through the water. By this stage we must be ready to drop the anchor immediately on his instruction. The pin through the bow roller should be out of the anchor shank and the anchor free to go; this may mean easing the anchor further out along the bow roller. We have carefully unwound the anchor chain that was around the cleat, but still have the chain running round the base of the cleat and held securely in both gloved hands. The chain may also be jammed against the side of the cleat by a foot (you are wearing sailing boots). The skipper says let go and we quickly, but under control, lower the anchor to the sea-bed, ie to the amount of chain we worked out was about right. It is surprisingly very difficult to judge, particularly in deeper water, when the anchor has hit the bottom. The anchor cable does not suddenly get lighter, as the weight of the chain hanging over the bow confuses things. As the boat begins to drift back in the wind we slowly pay out as much additional chain as the skipper asks, which is unlikely to be less than three times the depth of the water and then tie off the chain securely around the deck cleat.

The sails are dropped, life becomes less hectic and we can take in

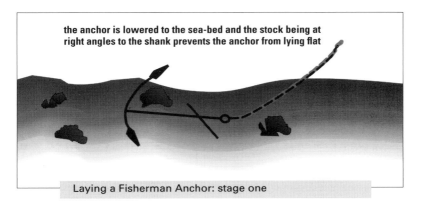

the anchor is lowered to the sea-bed and the stock being at
right angles to the shank prevents the anchor from lying flat

Laying a Fisherman Anchor: stage one

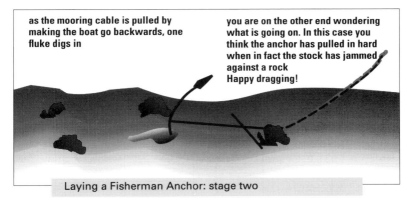

as the mooring cable is pulled by
making the boat go backwards, one
fluke digs in

you are on the other end wondering
what is going on. In this case you
think the anchor has pulled in hard
when in fact the stock has jammed
against a rock
Happy dragging!

Laying a Fisherman Anchor: stage two

our surroundings. This is not idle curiosity; we need to establish that the anchor has dug in and the boat is not drifting or dragging the anchor along the bottom.

The skipper is happy at last, and wants to go ashore. Can the crew blow up the dinghy while he finishes off entering the passage details in the log? His job you may note involves sitting down below in the warm and lifting a pencil; our job involves major physical exertion.

Oh, and could someone put up the anchor ball?

77

8
MOORINGS AND MARINAS

Our skipper chose to anchor for the night. Not that many do, preferring to pick up a mooring or go from marina berth to marina berth, which is a shame because they and their crew miss out on an essential and highly pleasurable part of sailing. As crew we must know what is expected of us in the common mooring and berthing situations: these are mooring alongside a pontoon; on a buoy; between piles; and the Mediterranean Moor. The objective in each situation is quite clear, but how it is to be achieved is not always so obvious as there are hidden forces at work, sometimes it may seem wilfully, preventing us from safely tying up the boat. It makes it much easier to understand what is required of us if we can understand what is going on in the skipper's head as he makes his decisions about what to do. And to understand that we need to know more about how a boat is controlled.

Steering

We drive down to the marina, which looks like a floating car park, jump on board, start the engine and drive off. It is easy to assume, especially if the boat has a ship's wheel as opposed to a tiller, that nothing has changed; and yet nothing is the same. You drive a car seated at the front. As you turn the wheel the very front of the car turns, the back follows. You have excellent visibility. You have precise steering control, precise acceleration, and precise braking, all of it instant. You do not have to take into account the weather. The ground is not moving, only you are. You do not need anyone else to help as you are in total control.

Compare this with a boat. You steer from the back and your visibility is hampered, not just by the mast but often by the people you need to help you. As you turn the wheel, it is not the front that turns but the back, which skews the boat sideways to begin with. The front keeps going more or less as before, at least at first. You have control over engine speed and whether you have the engine pushing the boat forward or back but the system is by no means so responsive; and there is a delay after the engine is actually put into reverse before you start going astern. The steering is very imprecise and your control over where the boat goes, no matter what you are doing with the wheel, is affected by wind, by the water under the boat which may be on the move, even by the boat's propeller going round under the boat as this kicks the boat's stern to one side or the other, depending on which way the propeller is going round. There are no brakes. As a consequence of all these factors, parking a boat is nothing like parking a car.

Imagine a car park with walls all round it. The spaces are very small and there is little room to turn. The spaces are not painted on the ground but are made by poles sticking out of the wall towards you. The car park is almost full. You enter the car park, see a space, and head towards it between the other cars' boots which stick out a long way beyond the poles. As you slow down you realise you have no brakes. The steering wheel suddenly seems soggy and even when you turn it hard the car only turns slowly. The wind comes up and you find despite turning the wheel and accelerating you still do not go in the direction of the space as for some reason the wind will not let you turn the front of the car towards the space. You tell your passengers that you are going to make an attempt to accelerate hard into the space but they must be ready to grab the poles either side to stop the car hitting the wall, if you make it, otherwise could they do their best to push the car away from the boots of the other cars if you miss. If you can try to add to this the idea that the ground may be moving as well, like a slow travelator at an airport, then you can see that skippers, even very experienced ones, get tense in marinas as the job is not easy and there is little room left for a mistake.

Apart from the boat handling skills of the skipper, success or failure rests with the crew. And it brings us back to handling ropes, as ropes are used not only as the brakes but also to help steer once we get to the final stage of mooring up.

Entering the Marina

The sails have been lowered and are tied up with sail ties. The halliards have NOT been taken off however, nor has the sail cover been put over the boom. Engines fail, usually at the most inconvenient time and often shortly after they have been started, not after they have been running well for several hours, and the chances are that the engine has only just been started to get into the marina. The skipper must have the option open to hoist a sail and get the boat under some sort of control quickly if the engine stops; the alternative of anchoring is not always possible eg in the entrance of a busy commercial harbour.

Three or four fenders are taken out of the cockpit locker along with the mooring warps; it is likely that four warps will be required. If the skipper knows which berth he is heading for in the marina and on which side the pontoon is going to be, we can tie on the fenders along the fattest part of that side of the boat using clove hitches (see diagram page 25), or round turns and two half hitches (see diagram page 23). These lines may have to be adjusted once in the marina and closer to the berth to ensure that the fenders are at the right height to stop the side of the boat hitting the pontoon as pontoons are not at one standard height.

79

There are also some interesting variations of pontoons but the two most common are long pontoons, where boats tie up one behind each other, and finger pontoons, where boats moor in pairs separated by a thin and often wobbly catwalk. It is quite common to have both in the same marina. You come alongside the holding pontoon, a long one, and stay there temporarily until allocated a vacant finger berth. If crowded, you may have to lie alongside another boat already tied on to the holding pontoon, and this can be repeated outside you and result in a line of boats extending out into the marina.

Whatever type of pontoon the skipper's job is to get the boat close enough to the pontoon for us as crew to step or jump a short distance onto the pontoon (not leap off, rope between our teeth trying for the world record long jump,) and take control over the situation with our excellent rope handling skills. What are we trying to achieve? We want to stop the boat from going forward, from going sideways away from the pontoon; and we also don't want the boat to be pushed back out of control by the wind or current. We are trying to establish control over forwards, sideways and backwards movement, all with ropes.

On all boats there are at least three mooring cleats, one at the bow, and one each side of the stern. There may well be two at the bow, there should be one each side amidships, and quite often the cockpit winches get brought into use for securing mooring warps. Just as boats have cleats, so do pontoons. The cleats are varied in design; we have to look ahead and see which sort are on the pontoons and prepare ourselves accordingly, and not take the ropes ashore and then stand scratching our heads as the boat drifts away.

Coming Alongside the Pontoon

We have got to go to the long, holding pontoon first. Right, we know which side the boat is going to be berthed so we can start tying the lines on the boat before we enter the marina. If we are berthing with the pontoon along our right, starboard, side, we are berthing *starboard side to*. The bow line can go on. This is tied to a cleat on the foredeck (front), led straight OUT through our fairlead and then back over the guard rails again. The part of the rope we take ashore is formed into a loose coil; we walk back towards the cockpit, just past the shrouds and sit on the coachroof, making sure we have passed the coiled part of the rope outside the shrouds on our way. The same happens with the stern line. It is made fast around the stern cleat on the right side of the boat, led out through the fairlead (if there is one), back over the guard rails, and taken forward towards the shrouds where we sit down so as not to block the view of the helmsman, who is by now tight lipped and running on neat adrenalin.

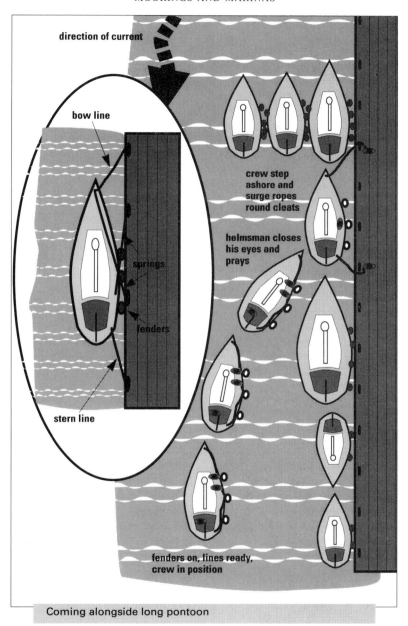

direction of current

bow line

crew step
ashore and
surge ropes
round cleats

helmsman closes
his eyes and
prays

springs

fenders

stern line

fenders on, lines ready,
crew in position

Coming alongside long pontoon

Long pontoons In the case of long pontoons, the space the helmsman is aiming for is only just a few feet longer than the boat itself. He has to come close past a boat moored before the space, sharply turn the boat into the space and get the boat close enough to the pontoon to enable us crew to take the bow and stern lines ashore and do it slowly enough to give us time to get the lines round the cleats and to take control. The faster he goes the more steerage he has, but the more he risks hitting the boat in front. Go too slow and he hasn't enough control to get the boat's nose far enough into the space to get the crew off, and if he gets the angle of approach wrong he may hit the boat behind the space.

As the final approach is made to the berth, trying hard not to obstruct the view of the helmsman, we get ready to go ashore. The crewmember with the bow line, stands up, holds onto one of the shrouds and gets ready to step onto the pontoon. It is not good practice, but regularly done, for crew to step over the guardrail, while still holding onto the shrouds, onto the *coaming* (top of the side of the joint between the hull and deck), along the side of the boat to make stepping onto the pontoon quicker and easier. As soon as the crew can safely reach the pontoon, stretching but not jumping, he or she takes the line ashore. The second crewmember follows close behind.

Now for the critical bit. It is not simply a matter of tying the end of rope in your hand to the first available cleat. In this initial stage you are not tying anything but controlling, and this is done by taking a turn of rope around the correct cleat, *surging* (letting it run round the cleat but under control) the rope safely and bringing the boat to a halt and along-side the pontoon.

If the pontoon is a long one, as in this case, then it is simply a matter of taking the bow line forward and surging it round a cleat, and the stern line backwards behind the boat and similarly surging it round a cleat. By adjusting these two lines, in a co-ordinated fashion you can move the boat backwards and forwards along the side of the pontoon until the skipper is happy the boat is in the correct place.

Finger pontoons With finger pontoons, it is unfortunately not a simple matter of taking the bow line to the cleat furthest away and the stern line to the stern cleat, as is shown in most diagrams, for the simple reason that the pontoon is shorter than the boat. This means that if you are trying to stop forward progress, the stern line is useless and so either the cleat halfway down the side deck or failing that a cockpit winch, has to come in to play. What is often required is a short line tied around the middle cleat on the boat. As the boat enters the berth this line is surged round the end cleat on the pontoon which stops forward progress.

Mooring lines Only once the boat has stopped and the position along the pontoon has been adjusted, can we finally make our lines fast to the cleats on the pontoon. We now need two extra lines to stop the boat gently rocking from side to side. These are called springs and can be secured as shown in the diagram. Different skippers have different methods, and anyway things have to be adjusted to take account of where the cleats are, both on the boat and the pontoon, but the principle is the same, you are stopping the boat from moving about.

THE MOST IMPORTANT POINTS TO REMEMBER ARE:

1 *Preparation*: It is too late to fumble with a line that has not been properly coiled when you step ashore.

2 *Be aware*: When you step onto the pontoon, that is only the beginning. Keep looking at what the boat is doing so that you take your line quickly to the correct cleat, not the first one you come to. Be aware also of what is happening with the other lines so you are not pulling against a crew member. Be aware of what is happening to the boat. If you pull too hard you can bang the boat's sides so hard against the pontoon that the fenders are pushed up, or accelerate the boat towards the next boat along, and if the stern line is not on, then it may be too late to stop the boat.

3 *Be safe*: Don't make a death defying leap towards the pontoon. Think of the consequences to you if you miss: it is not simply a matter of getting wet, but also that the skipper has no brakes he can apply to stop you being squashed between the boat and the pontoon. Handle rope properly. Always, but always, take a turn of the rope around the cleat before the load comes onto it. You do not have the strength on your own to stop a moving boat. Surge the line around a cleat and you have control, without needing huge muscles. And never ever take a turn of rope around your wrist to give you better grip.

Remember that the helmsman needs as much help as you can give him. If, when entering the marina, you don't know which side the boat is going to be brought alongside, whether starboard-side to or port-side to, then once the decision has been made which berth to go for, fenders and mooring lines go on quickly. Marinas are crowded places with lots of boats on the move, both big and small, many moving at absurd speeds, and you should be looking around the whole time and telling the helmsman what is going on, particularly in areas where his vision is blocked. It is so easy for your mind to switch off at the end of a day's sailing. The sails are down, the engine is on, the marina is in sight, thoughts are on everything from hot showers to has the bar shut, and the concentration of the crew goes as the chattering increases.

Mooring Buoys

It should come as no surprise that it is not just the difference in cost that makes many people choose to tie up to mooring buoys rather than get involved in waterborne dodgems in marinas. In comparison, tying up to a buoy is so much easier; for a start there is only one line. But it is a task which again requires skill on the part of both the helmsman and crew. Mooring buoys come in different guises but the principle is always the same. They are just large floats attached to the sea-bed by a long chain and lots of anchors; tie on to the buoy and you are in effect anchored.

The two most common situations are a mooring buoy with a large ring on the top and a mooring buoy with or without a ring but with another line already attached and connected to a *pick-up buoy* floating close by. The skipper's job is to get the boat close enough for the crew to be able either to pass a line through the ring on the top of the buoy or pick up the pick-up buoy. Well organised, it causes few problems.

Approaching Mooring Buoys

The helmsman has to slow the boat down gradually, taking into account the wind and the current so that the front of the boat comes to a halt beside the buoy. This may be done under engine or under sail. The task is not so easy if there are strong winds and/or currents pushing the boat away from the buoy. The two problems are that once the boat slows right down the helmsman has less control, and then for the last ten feet or so he or she cannot see the buoy; it is hidden from view by the boat's hull. At the bow, the crew's problem is one of reaching the buoy and then holding on long enough to pass a line through the ring and bring it back on board to tie off quickly to the foredeck cleat. There is rarely time actually to tie a knot around the ring of the buoy as the boat stays still only for a very short time. Before we get to the buoy, a strong line has to be secured to a foredeck cleat with the lazy or loose end ready to be threaded out through the fairlead, through the ring, and brought back on board. The line should be long enough to get to the buoy and back but not a great deal more than this.

A *boat hook* (a pole, usually wood but it can be plastic coated metal, such as aluminium, with a hook on the end) helps extend the crew's reach; using it the buoy can be pulled closer to the boat and upwards and then the line passed through the ring. Two crew make the task easier as one grabs with the boat hook and the other, already lying down on the foredeck reaches down with the mooring line.

Clearly co-ordination is required between the crew and the helmsman. The crew must be able, by some agreed set of hand signals, to direct the helmsman for the last vital ten feet or so, and also to let the helmsman know whether the buoy has in fact been picked up. It is common for the approach to be too fast. The crew successfully get the

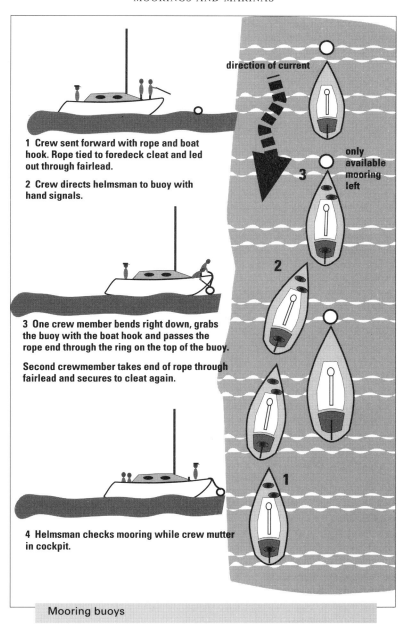

1 **Crew sent forward with rope and boat hook. Rope tied to foredeck cleat and led out through fairlead.**

2 **Crew directs helmsman to buoy with hand signals.**

direction of current

3

only available mooring left

2

3 **One crew member bends right down, grabs the buoy with the boat hook and passes the rope end through the ring on the top of the buoy.**

Second crewmember takes end of rope through fairlead and secures to cleat again.

1

4 **Helmsman checks mooring while crew mutter in cockpit.**

Mooring buoys

85

boat hook through the ring but the boat is moving so fast that the crewmember simply cannot stop the boat's progress. This is when accidents happen because understandably the crew does not want to let the side down and let go of the buoy, or worse lose the boat hook. Life is not so short that there is not time to go round again if the first attempt fails, and boat hooks are just broom handles with a cheap metal fitting on the end; they can be replaced with much less pain than waiting for a broken arm to mend.

Hand signals are used rather than shouts because the helmsman can hear very little back in the cockpit if the engine is on or the sails are flapping about, and as crew you tend to look forwards towards the buoy. So shouting 'ten feet, go left, no left, left, five feet, two feet' straight at the buoy may frighten away any seagulls sitting on it, but will be of no help to the helmsman.

Some boats' *topsides* (the bit above water up to deck level) are so high, especially at the bow, that it may be impossible to reach the buoy coming in nose-on, and then the helmsman has to get the boat at rest with the buoy nearer to the shrouds where the deck will be closer to the water. This makes the skipper nervous because there is a danger that the line going down from the buoy to the sea-bed will get caught round the keel or round the propeller.

Approaching Pick-up Buoys

Mooring buoys with their own smaller pick-up buoys attached are easier targets. Once you have grabbed the pick-up buoy with the boat hook, the smaller buoy is quickly dragged up onto the foredeck and pulled in. You do not tie on with the light line attached to the pick-up buoy, but keep pulling and then a more substantial rope or loop of chain will appear and this is what is made fast around the deck cleat. As with mooring alongside, once the line has gone through the ring and been brought back on board quickly pass it round a cleat before the load comes on and you will have control. Don't stand up with the line coming straight from the buoy to your hands; you are unlikely to be able to hold on, even if the boat is only moving very slowly. With the line securely tied off, and the boat still, the skipper may then decide to attach a second line, or adjust the length of the line.

There is another situation you will come across where you find two mooring buoys being used, one with a line to go on the bow and one or two to go on the stern, called mooring *fore and aft*, which we will look at shortly.

Pile Moorings

In river estuaries, and some small yacht harbours, you will find rows of large poles sticking vertically out of the water with yachts strung between them. Boats are secured *fore and aft* (front and back) between the poles. This prevents the boats swinging round in the tide and lying across the river or harbour. It is easy to see what is required but not so easy to do. The task is easiest when the tide and wind are both in the same direction as an imaginary line drawn between the poles. If the wind is blowing crossways between the poles it is far from easy. The helmsman is totally dependant on the crew and they can make the task impossible. There are three basic options.

Method one The boat is taken carefully alongside the first pile. A line is passed through a metal ring attached to the pile or around the whole pile. The boat now motors to the second pile and a line is passed through another ring. The boat is pulled gently back by the stern line while the bow line is paid out to get the boat in between the piles.

Method two The boat is taken to the pile furthest away and a line secured. The boat drops back on this line so that the second pile can be reached and a line passed around it. The boat is pulled gently forward.

The helmsman cannot do the impossible. If there is any wind, or tide flowing under the boat, it is difficult to hold the boat stopped alongside the piles and yet this has to be done twice. There is every likelihood of the wind or tide taking control of the boat leaving the helmsman with the task of trying to regain steerage way, which he won't be able to do once the boat is tied to a pile. The crew need to be ready, all lines fed correctly, and aware of what will be required of them if things start to go slightly wrong.

A long line is attached to the stern cleat, taken outside through the fairlead and forward beyond the shrouds, possibly to the bow. As the first pile is approached the person with the stern line has to be ready either to feed the end of the line through a ring on the post, or to feed it around or even over the top of the post. A hand is raised to say this has been done and the helmsman can continue motoring towards the next pile. As the boat goes forward the stern line is carefully slipped through the ring making sure the rope does not catch on anything or dangle in the water. It is essential that no pull is exerted on the rope otherwise the helmsman no longer has any control of the boat.

The boat keeps going forward to the next pile; all the time the stern line is being paid out and the next line, which has been tied to a cleat on the foredeck and passed out through the fairlead, is passed through the ring and a hand is raised so the helmsman knows it has been a success. It is now up to the crew to middle the boat between the piles. If there is a problem with either of the lines the helmsman has to be told immediately as usually the only way out of the situation is to cast off the lines quickly and start again. One common problem is that the lines are too short to reach from the boat to the pile and back again, which is only discovered at a very late stage in the proceedings. The crew must be quick, make sure the lines do not snag, must not pull on the lines until asked to, and never cleat off any line until the exercise is finished.

It may not be possible to achieve the manoeuvre because of the conditions and it is no disgrace, in fact it is better seamanship in such circumstances, to use method three.

Method three The bow or stern of the boat is taken up to the first pile and a line attached and then the boat is allowed to hang a short distance off the pile. The dinghy is launched and the line to the second pile is rowed over and attached. The boat is then pulled into position. It may not be just the wind or tide that forces this course of action; the presence of other craft moored to the next set of piles may prevent the helmsman from being able to manoeuvre the boat close enough to one of the piles.

Trotted Moorings

Instead of piles, you might have to moor the boat between two mooring buoys. So you approach the first buoy, slip the line through the ring on the top, motor gently forwards to the next buoy, slip the line through the ring and then centre the boat. It helps to have two crew ready, one with a boat hook and one lying down or at least crouching on the side deck. The first buoy is hooked, the line passed through by the person lying down and back up to the person with the boat hook. The person lying down jumps up, takes the line and walks to the back of the boat paying out line if necessary. The person with the boat hook goes to the bow and gets ready to catch the next mooring where another crewmember is waiting with the forward line (this becomes an interesting exercise when short of crew).

If you are lucky, stretched between the piles or between the buoys will be a light line with a small buoy on it. Heave the light line on board and you will find heavier bow and stern lines ready to hook on. If you are unlucky the line between the buoys may be just under the surface and although you don't find it, the propeller always does.

The Mediterranean Moor

Remember the anchor kept in a bucket on the stern. It is common practice in the Mediterranean to moor a boat nose first to a quay wall, the stern held out at 90° by the anchor. The idea is that you motor towards the wall, drop the anchor off the stern and then keep going slowly towards the wall paying out the anchor chain. You nose up to the wall and a crewmember takes one or two lines ashore, that have first been attached to a foredeck cleat, and secures them around bollards or metal rings. By pulling in on the anchor chain the boat's bow can be pulled clear from the wall and yet when you want to go ashore you just pull on the bow lines until you are close enough to step ashore. It takes no imagination to see the possibilities for little errors creeping in to this procedure, but if you go flotilla sailing this is the norm and you soon get the hang of it.

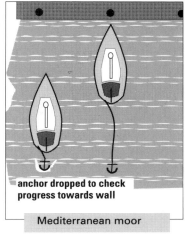

anchor dropped to check progress towards wall

Mediterranean moor

No Moorings Available

Moorings and marina berths are always in short supply where you want them and when you want them. This means it is common practice to moor up alongside another boat. This is no different in principle from mooring alongside a pontoon, only it is a bit more difficult for the crew as the pontoon is curved and cluttered up with lots of gear, even people. The same principles apply of having the fenders at the right height, ropes ready, an idea of where the lines are to be attached, being aware of what is happening to the boat and what other crew members are doing, but most of all concentrating on the job in hand.

There are common courtesies that should be followed. If the boat is occupied ask whether it is all right to come alongside. Don't swing yourself on board using their shrouds; out of your sight down below, someone could at that moment be pouring boiling water out of a kettle. Don't crash about and shout a lot, the crew on board may have just got to sleep after a long overnight passage. If you can, it is better to take your own stern lines and bow lines ashore to avoid straining the fittings on the inside boat but this is done only after you have secured yourself alongside the inside boat.

Finally two important rules: when going ashore across another boat always, but always, go round the front of the mast, never through the cockpit as this severely invades the privacy of the other crew; and try and find out what the intentions are of the inside boat. Don't just tie up and walk away. They may have to leave at a certain time to catch a tide and if they are delayed too long, because you are wandering about in town, they may lose not a few hours but a whole day of their holiday.

9
CHARTS AND PUBLICATIONS

We left our crew at anchor getting ready to go ashore. The skipper put up an anchor light as well as the ball, as he suspected that they would be ashore all evening. He also asked his crew to take their lifejackets ashore, which they all refused to do, protesting they were strong swimmers, the sea was calm and the shore was less than fifty yards away. The skipper said nothing but when no one was looking he quietly slipped them in the bottom of the going-ashore bag anyway.

After a convivial evening, the skipper and crew returned to the dinghy and found that quite a chop had come up as the tide was now going the opposite way to the wind. Although many jokes were made at the skipper's expense, all donned their lifejackets before setting off in the dark to try and work out which of the numerous anchor lights was theirs. Finally the dinghy was brought alongside the right yacht and secured, and then one by one the crew clambered on board ready for their bunks.

In the morning, after a late breakfast, the VHF radio was switched on and out came the charts, the almanacs and local pilots as plans were made for the day.

Charts

The amount of information charts contain is extraordinary; they are not simply contour maps of the sea-bed. Charts show the coastline and conspicuous objects ashore, they show what is completely under the surface of the water, what sticks up out of the water all the time, and what is sometimes out of the water and sometimes underneath it, depending on the tide. Charts show the state of the sea-bed, the direction and strength of the currents in the water for every hour, navigational marks such as buoys, beacons and lighthouses, which buoys have lights on them, what colour the lights are, whether they flash on and off, and if they do how fast they flash. Charts also show anchorages, moorings, shipping lanes reserved for big ships, areas where the sea may be exceptionally rough; the list goes on and on. To compress all this information onto one piece of paper requires the use of lots of symbols and codes which take time to learn, but can easily be looked up in a reference book if needs be. The almanacs contain the principal codes and symbols but it is far better to use a separate publication produced by the Admiralty which provides comprehensive information in an easily accessible form.

Charts also provide an accurate base for navigation so that a line drawn

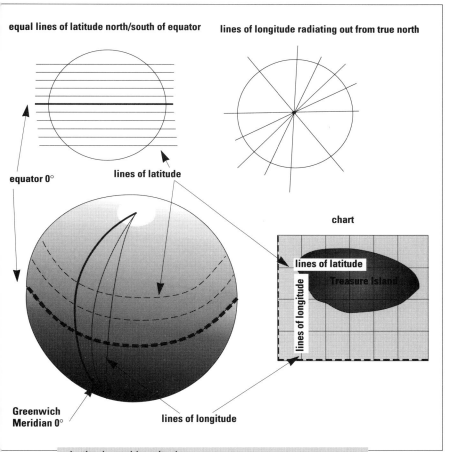

equal lines of latitude north/south of equator

lines of longitude radiating out from true north

equator 0°

lines of latitude

chart

lines of latitude

Treasure Island

lines of longitude

Greenwich
Meridian 0°

lines of longitude

Latitude and longitude

on a chart can represent accurately the distance between two objects at sea. This is far more difficult to achieve than might be realised. We know the earth is more or less round (an obloid spheroid) but we perceive things to be flat. We also need a flat piece of paper to put on a flat chart table to do our navigation with flat instruments; yet we are sailing over a curved surface.

To start with, the earth is divided up into a grid with horizontal and vertical lines. The horizontal lines on the map, called lines of *latitude*, are all drawn parallel with the equator. The line at the equator is numbered 0, and the parallel lines drawn north and south of this are numbered from 1 to 90.

Southern England is between 50 and 51, written as 50°N and 51°N. A series of vertical lines on the map, called lines of *longitude*, drawn from the north pole to the south pole, 360 in all, provide the other reference, and they are numbered as 0 to 180 East or West of the Greenwich Meridian; this is an imaginary line that runs from the north pole through England at Greenwich Observatory and on to the south pole. The diagram on page 91 makes this much clearer. By reference to these lines of longitude and latitude we can describe our position anywhere on the globe. Charts are drawn with the lines of longitude going up the sides and lines of latitude across from side to side.

But to draw a chart, first the curved surface has to be accurately surveyed, then the information obtained drawn out as though it was really a flat surface. This is achieved by a complex mathematical calculation called a projection and there is a variety of these in use.

The relevance of all of this to us, apart from impressing us immensely, is that distances when drawn on a chart have to deliberately distorted. That means it is not possible to draw a scale at the bottom of the chart, say 30cm = 1 nautical mile, which can then be used for measuring distance across the whole of the chart. Instead a sort of distorted scale is provided, down either vertical edge of the chart. If you want to measure the length of a line drawn on a chart, you use the scale that is at the same position on the side of the chart.

The nautical mile itself has a fascinating history, and strictly defined is a different length at different parts of the globe. Various attempts have been made to agree a standard nautical mile and it has been different lengths even this century. In 1929 an international standard was adopted of 1,852 metres (approximately 6,076ft) which compares with a statute or land mile of 1,609.3m (5,280ft).

While on measurements we may mention that a fathom is 6ft and a cable is approximately one tenth of a nautical mile; the reasons why are rooted in history. It sounds very nautical to talk in fathoms and cables but nobody will really know what on earth you mean – these terms are best left for the yacht club bar.

The Admiralty, or more correctly the Hydrographer of the Navy, produces charts and maritime publications that cover the globe and are used everywhere by merchant shipping. The care that goes into preparing them, checking them and keeping them constantly up to date, can only be appreciated by visiting the Hydrographer's premises at Taunton, Somerset. Charts are drawn to all sorts of different scales, so that a standard full sized Admiralty Chart, which measures approximately 0.75 × 1.04 metres (28in × 42in) may indicate anything from say Plymouth Harbour to the whole of the British Isles. Until fairly recently Admiralty charts were prepared primarily with the needs of commercial shipping in mind but over the last ten years or so many charts have been adapted to include information for yachtsmen; and now special publications geared more towards small boats' needs are being produced.

Other charts exist, drawn specifically with the yachtsman in mind, such as those produced by *Imray, Norie and Wilson*, and *Barnacle Marine*. These are not separately surveyed but take as their base the information first produced by the Admiralty. The information is reworked and presented in a different style. These charts may be smaller and have more colours, and they may even be waterproof.

A recent development has been the production of charts on compact disks which are fed into an on-board computer-based navigation system. Depending on the sophistication of the system, you can sit down below at the navigation station, switch on your colour monitor, call up a chart at whatever scale you like, and superimposed on the screen will be your present position, which direction you are heading in and at what speed. The information base again comes from the charts produced by the Hydrographer of the Navy.

And then in addition there are many other nautical publications, such as pilots, cruising guides and the almanacs, that will have small charts in them.

Nautical Almanacs

Like the charts, nautical almanacs contain vast amounts of information, hence their large size and cost. A substantial chunk of an almanac is given over to tidal information given in the form of tables, graphs and little charts with arrows all over them. Why are we so interested in what the tide is doing?

The sea does not stay at the same height. Each day the level of the sea changes; it may rise, then drop, then rise again and then drop, each part of the sequence taking normally a little over 6 hours. This is not a constant around the whole coast; there are marked variations in certain locations such as Poole Harbour on the South Coast which has most peculiar tides with two high waters to each cycle not just one; and the almanac shows this also.

The amount the sea goes up and down each day also changes. There are lots of places we can get to only when the tide has reached a certain height, and lots of places we cannot stay if the tide is going to fall. We can take the tide as it *floods* (flows inwards or inland) up an estuary that does not have much water at low water, have lunch and then come back down again on the *ebb* (the tide flowing out to sea again). The forces at work causing all these changes are complex.

The main driving force is the moon which pulls the water in the oceans towards it. The success with which it does this varies throughout each month and throughout the year. The highest high water and lowest low water – they come as pairs together – called *spring* tides, occur about two days after a full moon. When the moon has the least effect, the tides do not rise so far or fall so far, and these are called *neap* tides.

It might be reasonable to suppose that the tide would rise and fall the same amount say along the length of the south coast or east coast but the variation in time, and height, and the direction that the water flows in, is enormous, even in locations adjacent to each other; hence our skipper's interest in what is happening to the tide today, where he is now and where he is going as well. The almanac gives this information to the skipper usually in the following form:

FALMOUTH Lat. 50°09'N. Long. 5°03'W.

HIGH & LOW WATER 1993

G.M.T.   ADD 1 HOUR MARCH 28-OCTOBER 24 FOR B.S.T.

SEPTEMBER				OCTOBER				NOVEMBER			
Time	m	Time	m	Time	m	Time	m	Time	m	Time	m
1 0516 1155 W 1728 ○	4.9 0.7 5.2	**16** 0506 1135 TH 1722 ●	5.4 0.1 5.7	**1** 0518 1159 F 1731	5.1 0.8 5.2	**16** 0525 1157 SA 1744	5.6 0.1 5.7	**1** 0011 0558 M 1229 1815	0.9 5.2 1.0 5.1	**16** 0047 0635 TU 1310 1859	0.4 5.5 0.5 5.3
2 0015 0546 TH 1229 1758	0.6 5.0 0.7 5.2	**17** 0000 0548 F 1219 1804	0.0 5.5 0.0 5.8	**2** 0014 0549 SA 1228 1803	0.7 5.2 0.8 5.2	**17** 0020 0608 SU 1241 1829	0.1 5.7 0.1 5.6	**2** 0040 0632 TU 1259 1848	1.0 5.1 1.1 4.9	**17** 0130 0717 W 1353 1943	0.7 5.4 0.7 5.0
3 0047 0616 F 1258 1828	0.6 5.0 0.7 5.2	**18** 0043 0629 SA 1301 1847	0.0 5.6 0.0 5.7	**3** 0041 0620 SU 1254 1835	0.8 5.1 0.9 5.1	**18** 0103 0651 M 1324 1913	0.2 5.6 0.3 5.4	**3** 0110 0702 W 1329 1920	1.1 5.0 1.2 4.8	**18** 0212 0758 TH 1436 2026	1.0 5.1 1.1 4.7
4 0113 0646 SA 1324 1858	0.8 5.0 0.9 5.0	**19** 0124 0710 SU 1342 1930	0.1 5.5 0.2 5.5	**4** 0106 0652 M 1320 1905	1.0 5.0 1.1 4.9	**19** 0145 0733 TU 1407 1958	0.6 5.3 0.7 5.1	**4** 0141 0733 TH 1402 1954	1.3 4.9 1.3 4.6	**19** 0253 0837 F 1520 2109	1.3 4.9 1.3 4.5
5 0138 0717 SU 1349 1929	0.9 4.9 1.0 4.9	**20** 0204 0752 M 1424 2015	0.4 5.3 0.5 5.1	**5** 0131 0721 TU 1346 1935	1.1 4.9 1.2 4.7	**20** 0227 0816 W 1451 2045	1.0 5.1 1.1 4.7	**5** 0215 0810 F 1440 2037	1.3 4.7 1.4 4.4	**20** 0337 0916 SA 1606 2156	1.6 4.6 1.6 4.2
6 0202	1.1	**21** 0245	0.8	**6** 0157	1.3	**21** 0311	1.3	**6** 0256	1.5	**21** 0424	1.9

Extract from almanac (Reed's)

As you can see he has the times of high and low waters. Care has to be taken that in British Summer Time, the extra hour is added to the times given in the almanac to get to the time shown on our watches.

The depths given for high and low water have to be added to the depths shown on the chart to arrive at the actual figure for the day. So if the chart says we are anchored in 3 metres, and at the time of low water the almanac says there will be 1.5 metres, this is added to the 3 metres on the chart. This particular sum applies of course for low water only. As the tide rises so does the amount of water under the boat at the anchorage. The charts and the almanac both use the same reference level (they have to or they would not work) called *Lowest Astronomical Tide*, which is the lowest level it is predicted that the tide might ever fall under normal conditions.

Enormous confusion can arise when a minus sign is used. It is common to see on a chart, say of a river estuary, figures given with minus signs on either side of the river. All this means is that for some of the time the river bank is exposed to view, while at other times it may be covered with water. If a mud bank is shown as having a depth of -1.5m, and low water for that day is 1.0m, then 0.5m of the mud bank will be sticking up out of the water at low water; and as the tide comes in and the water level rises, the mud disappears from view.

If our skipper wants to go over a shallow mud patch he must work out when there will be sufficient water under the boat, enough for us to cross over the mud without the keel getting stuck. He knows how much water he needs under the boat to keep it afloat, because that remains constant, he knows from the chart what the level of the mud bank is, and he can find out from the almanac when the tide will have risen enough that particular day to enable him to sail over the bank. It is depressingly easy to get the sum wrong, even though it is the simplest of calculations, so for this and other reasons, most skippers add in a large safety margin and do not take their boat over a mud bank when there is only just enough water, but only when there is bound to be enough.

Tides are affected by many forces other than the moon, not the least being the weather, which can alter the speed with which a tide rises, how high it gets and how quickly it goes out again. Not only is this true, it is a wonderful excuse for the skipper if he gets his sums wrong. As you can see, although the information given in almanacs is very detailed it has to be used with caution.

Local Pilots and Guides

Our skipper has decided that he wants us to sail from Plymouth for about 25 miles due west to the next safe harbour, Fowey. He has worked out the course he wants to go and written that down on the chart (how he does this will be explained shortly). Now he wants to find out more about the entrance to Fowey; such as, are there restrictions as to when he can get in to the harbour because of sandbanks, what navigational marks will he see outside the harbour, and what signs or marks should he follow as he enters the harbour. He also wants to know as much as possible about the facilities available in the harbour, where he can moor, what type of moorings are available, can he anchor, is there a water taxi service, where can he get fuel, where can everyone get showers and so on and so on.

Some of the information is on the chart, the almanac contains a great deal more and has its own little chart of the entrance but our skipper has also purchased a local pilot, in this case the *West Country Cruising Guide*, which gives him a chart of the entrance in colour, detailed descriptions of all the facilities afloat and ashore, and best of all photographs. He can see what to expect. One good photograph can put all the information immediately into context. Similar guides, in one form or another, exist for most areas regularly used by yachts.

Passage Planning

The skipper writes down in the ship's log the times of high and low waters he needs for the day and then gets out the charts of the area we want to get to. He draws a line or lines, avoiding all dangers, from where we are to where we want to get to. He measures along the lines to work out the distance and looks to see which way the water is flowing and how fast. He does this by finding out from the almanac whether the currents are running strongly today or not, and in which direction. The currents mimic the tides in that they flow one way for so long, then turn and flow roughly the opposite way.

Although it is not apparent on board, boats move very slowly, four nautical miles per hour being quite reasonable, and for most cruising yachts under 10 metres long their maximum will be around 7 knots. The importance of the tidal streams and their rates is easy to comprehend if you just think of the tides as escalators. You can have no sails up at all and still move along at 2 knots if that is what the tide is doing. The water is carrying you along with it on the escalator. Now turn round and try to go the other way. You have to go at least 2 knots just to stay still. You are running the wrong way up the escalator.

After his deliberations and much pencil sucking, the skipper informs us that we will be sailing approximately due south to begin with, about 185° Compass until we are well clear of Rame Head, and then when we have fixed our position using the handbearing compass, we will turn on to 280° Compass. Early Greek again.

10
COMPASSES

Our skipper, having done his sums, plots the course he wants to follow on the chart. He does this using even more information given on the chart concerning compasses. And if ever there was a subject that the average person, such us you and I, was designed not to understand, it is compasses. The idea is simple, but confusion reigns on-board once they are put into use.

How a Compass Works

A magnetised needle, balanced and allowed to rotate will always come to rest with the needle pointing north/south. The needle aligns itself along the earth's magnetic field. There is a magnetic north pole, slightly off from the geographic north pole, and the north point of a compass always points to that spot. As a magnetised needle will always point in the same direction, if we put it inside a bowl or dish and mark out a scale or reference numbers all round the inside then we can work out where we are relative to the north pole (see diagram page 98). We point our compass bowl in one direction, the needle swings round to point towards north, and now we can count the numbers round the inside of the bowl to work out the difference between where north is and where we are facing.

The system of measurement is a dial or circle divided up into 360 units called *degrees*. But:

1 true north or geographic north is different from magnetic north;

2 the position of magnetic north changes, albeit slowly, all the time;

3 any other magnetic field near to the compass needle will cause a distortion. This may be caused by the geology of the earth or, closer to home, equipment on the boat. Boats are full of metal bits and innumerable items of electronic equipment, which may confuse matters by only causing a problem when they are switched on;

4 charts are drawn with their vertical lines pointing towards the geographic north pole, not the magnetic north pole.

Yet it is essential for us to be able to draw a line on a chart, say from Eddystone Lighthouse to Falmouth, and be able to steer the boat along it somehow, perhaps in fog when we cannot see anything at all.

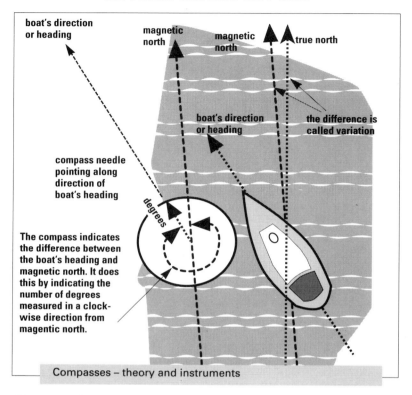

boat's direction or heading

magnetic north

magnetic north

true north

boat's direction or heading

the difference is called variation

compass needle pointing along direction of boat's heading

degrees

The compass indicates the difference between the boat's heading and magnetic north. It does this by indicating the number of degrees measured in a clock-wise direction from magentic north.

Compasses – theory and instruments

Compass Courses

Let us start with the idea of direction being described as an angle. We are familiar with the directions north, south, east and west but direction can also be described like a clock where the whole circle of the clock face is divided up into 360 divisions, the degrees of a compass. If we are at the centre of the clock we can describe a direction simply by using the degree that corresponds with where we want to go. If we want to go east, that is 90°, a bit further round, 100° and so on; so using a circle of degrees we can describe any direction very accurately.

It would be wonderfully convenient if a compass needle pointed to true north wherever we happened to be. We could always work out which way were facing simply by looking at the compass. The needle would face north and we could count the degrees' difference between the way it was pointing and where we were headed. And that is exactly what we do on a boat using the ship's compass, which is in a fixed position, and a hand-bearing compass, which is portable. Only we have to take account of the regrettable facts of life that the compass points to magnetic north not true north, and that it is so readily susceptible to bribes from other stray magnetic fields.

Compass Rose

On the chart will be at least one, usually several, compass roses. A compass rose is a degrees clock, with the degrees marked off round the edges of the circle. There is insufficient room to give each number, so you will see the clock face numbered say every 5°.

The start, 0°, and finish, 360°, is at the top. The clock is arranged with the 0° pointing towards true north. Superimposed over this may be another compass rose rotated, so that the 0° points towards

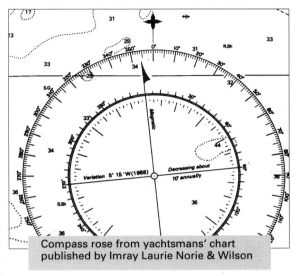

Compass rose from yachtsmans' chart published by Imray Laurie Norie & Wilson

magnetic north. Right, we now have both true north and magnetic north.

Our compasses on board point towards magnetic north. We are steering straight towards Eddystone lighthouse which we can see is dead ahead and our ship's compass says is 95°Compass. We can come down to the chart table, and find Eddystone lighthouse marked on the chart. We find our compass rose, look at the magnetic rose and draw a line from the centre of the rose outwards to the 95° mark and beyond. But the line does not go through the lighthouse, it just continues across the chart missing the lighthouse by miles. This is because wherever we are at sea, we just do not happen to be in the middle of the compass rose. However we know we are pointing down a line of 95°C (Compass) and we can see the lighthouse dead ahead, so the line must go through the lighthouse (and if there are no stray magnetic fields around it will). So if we could only shift the line drawn from the centre of the compass at 95°M (Magnetic) so that it stayed pointing 95°M but went through the lighthouse on the chart we would know we were somewhere along that line. And we can do this easily with a variety of plotting instruments, the simplest to understand straightaway being parallel rules, which are simply two rulers hinged together. You put one edge of one ruler against your 95°M line, swing the other ruler out until it goes through the lighthouse and we can draw our 95°M line again. We are somewhere along this line.

Now if we could just find something else to point the boat at and take another compass reading, another *bearing*, we could plot that one as well. The lines must cross because we are pointing the boat in different directions. And they must cross where we are, because we are at the one and only spot that the different views, the different compass bearings, can be seen and taken. If we move the boat say half a mile then the bearings will change. For some this information will be fascinating, others as welcome as a party political broadcast; but for those less inclined to be interested, stick with it for a few more minutes and you will soon see how it affects you as competent crew, apart from boring you rigid.

Course to Steer

If our skipper wants to steer the boat in a particular direction, say from Eddystone to Falmouth, he can draw a line between the two places on the chart. He can then check this line against the nearest compass rose and find out what the direction is as a compass reading. He writes this down. We get out to the Eddystone and turn for Falmouth, but we cannot see Falmouth, it is too far away. But the skipper knows that once he is on the line the ship's compass will show the same figure as the one he worked out. He can then tell the crew to steer say 275° by the ship's compass, and retire below out of the rain again. Providing we keep the boat's nose pointing along that line we will get to Falmouth, in due course.

What the skipper has to be wary of, apart from our ability to steer a course just by looking at the compass, which does take some practice, is other magnetic fields on the boat which may cause the compass to *deviate*. Fixed magnetic influences on the boat can be adjusted out on the compass or allowed for in the skipper's calculations. It is the random ones that cause major problems, such as a crew member putting his can of drink near the compass or leaning over the compass with his Walkman on.

So as competent crew we should be aware of the importance of not causing the compass to deviate, understand how important the compass is, and be able to steer a particular course by the compass; and help in navigating the ship by using the hand-bearing compass.

Hand-bearing Compass

It is inconvenient to keep turning the boat's nose towards conspicuous objects on the land or lighthouses at sea in order to be able to take bearings and plot our position. Instead we use a small hand-bearing compass for this job. Again it gives magnetic readings in the form of degrees and again we have to be aware of the magnetic influence that other objects might have on the compass and not prop it up on the coachroof with a beer can for example. Simply by taking two or three bearings of objects we can see and that are also shown on the chart, we can draw out these bearings on the chart and where the lines cross is approximately where we are. There is always a certain amount of operator error so the lines don't cross exactly, and they may form a triangle if three lines are used. This is called a *cocked hat*. So if the skipper asks you to take some bearings and you call them down to him at the chart table (where he rests still out of the rain) and if when he has plotted them out he starts muttering about cocked hats three miles wide, he has not gone delirious.

Electronic Position Fixing

Many modern electronic navigation systems now commonly in use on yachts describe the boat's position very accurately indeed. They do this either by the use of radio beacons sited on the coast, or by bouncing signals off satellites. Their accuracy is excellent, they consume little power, the readings are continuous and are available instantly at the touch of a button. Such technological developments have revolutionised small boat sailing and have made it, in most circumstances, much safer. So why bother with a compass and traditional navigation?

Skill in reading a ship's compass and being able to steer a course by it, and the ability to take a bearing quickly with a hand-bearing compass are still essential skills for several reasons; first, the land-based signal stations and the satellites that beam out signals are shut down from time to time for maintenance and repair purposes; second, there is the possibility of power failure (although some of the latest satellite systems have a limited built-in battery back-up facility); third, equipment does fail, especially in the harsh marine environment with its salt water atmosphere; fourth, but much less common, a lightning strike may wipe out all electronic instruments; fifth, much essential navigation and pilotage information is given in terms of compass bearings eg the entrance to a harbour may have rocks either side, or even in the middle of it, and it is only by steering specific compass courses that you will miss the rocks; and sixth, the compass information is instantly available in the cockpit, whereas you may have to go below and start pushing buttons to get the display up that you need to see on the electronic system and, if tense, you are likely to push the wrong button.

Enough of all this stuff. The weather has come over the VHF, and been written down in the log as: S 3 to 4, vis mod to good, no warnings, sea slight. The skipper seems happy, so it's time to get the boat underway and on passage to Fowey.

11
SAFETY ON BOARD

Before we head off out to sea for the first time, it might be a prudent time to spend a few moments on safety. The business of going ashore in the dinghy raises some interesting points. The actions of the skipper in first asking us crew to take lifejackets ashore, our refusal to do so, and his quietly putting the jackets in the going-ashore bag all the same, raise three basic problem areas about safety at sea that have to be faced on all cruising boats: how far is the skipper responsible for the safety of the crew, how much responsibility lies with the crew to look after their own safety, and the differing perceptions of what is a dangerous situation.

You must work out your own answers to the first two problems. A cruising boat is not subject to naval discipline, the crew are 'willing volunteers'; but that clearly does not absolve the skipper from having a duty of care. And yet in this case his safety advice was ridiculed. The real problem is the differing perceptions of what is a potentially dangerous situation.

Perception of Danger

When beginning sailing it is easy to think that the most dangerous situation must be when the sea is rough, especially if you have read many of the 'dismasted in Atlantic gale' type of article, popular in the yachting press. An experienced skipper is quite relaxed in strong winds offshore, or when the wind is blowing hard off the land. The boat may be reefed down just to one small sail, the seas up to two metres high, the occasional wave may even be breaking near the boat and yet the skipper will still be reasonably relaxed out at sea, whereas an inexperienced crew member will be thinking his time has come and why did he ever agree to go to the Channel Islands on his friends' yacht.

When they close the coast and start to make their approach towards St Peter Port, the crewmember's spirits will soar; inside he will be saying to himself, 'I can see land, we are saved', and may ask the skipper how much longer will it be before they are in harbour. He should not be surprised at having his head bitten off by a skipper who is now decidedly tense. The skipper knows that the most dangerous part of the passage is coming up and he has to get the boat in exactly the right place; there is little room for error now. The seas may even begin to subside a little depending on the direction of the wind and the currents, but his concentration needs to be one hundred per cent. He will only relax when the boat is securely tied to a buoy in the harbour.

To some extent as competent crew we need therefore to take the advice of more experienced crew and the skipper. If their view of a situation is that it is potentially dangerous, it might well be prudent to accept their advice and put on a lifejacket or safety harness. But we still need to have some view of our own as to what is a dangerous situation. We also have to learn practical skills on how to look after ourselves on board, and how to summon help in an emergency.

Safety on Board

This can be divided into two categories, personal safety and boat safety. Although crew, and not skipper, we still have responsibilities in both areas.

Personal safety

It is clearly in our own interests not to get damaged or fall out of the boat or, worse still, both. There are practical measures we can take to reduce the risks but the critical factor is our own attitude. To be safe, you have to think safe. The right attitude starts with such simple things as using ropes safely so you don't damage your hands; and not standing up when the boat is about to gybe. This entails no more than us being aware of what is going on around. Even keeping warm and dry by wearing the right sort of clothing makes a major contribution to personal safety. But once we start moving around the boat, even in moderate seas, it is important to get used to putting on a safety harness and to clipping on.

Safety harnesses

There are many varieties of safety harness about, and some are now built into wet weather sailing jackets. A safety harness is made of strong webbing, and has buckles to adjust the size of the chest and shoulder straps which meet at a heavy metal fitting in front of the chest where another line is attached which has safety hooks on both ends. For a harness to be of any use, first you have to adjust it to fit your size (it should be reasonably tight, not loose) and second you must clip the safety line onto a secure fitting on the boat. And you clip on when you feel unsafe, or when the skipper asks you to.

In quite moderate conditions with waves less than one metre, even in the relative security of the cockpit, it is still advisable to clip on when the boat is *hard-on-the-wind* (going close-hauled and therefore leaning over) or tacking, as it is easy to lurch from the uphill side of the cockpit to the downhill and continue your progress out over the side. In moderate conditions you should always clip on when going out of the cockpit, whether going up to the mast to reef, or up to the foredeck to change sails, to free off a sheet caught round a hatch or whatever. You should clip on, even when in a hurry.

Running up each side of the boat on the deck, or occasionally along the coachroof, there should be a wire or length of webbing called a *jackstay* for you to clip onto. If not, fix one yourself using a mooring warp or spare sheet. It only takes a few minutes to rig one up (which should have been rigged in harbour). You simply clip your safety line to the jackstay and then you can move up to the mast knowing that if you trip or fall for any reason, you are still tied on to the boat. The line does not prevent you getting hurt, it does not help you keep your feet on a bouncing deck – 'one hand for the boat and one for yourself' is the much repeated maxim which simply means keep holding on at least with one hand, quite often an impossibility – it merely prevents you from parting company with the boat.

You always go forward on the uphill side of the boat, so that if you fall, you fall into the boat and not out of it, whether clipped on or not. And even in slight seas it is advisable to crouch rather than stand. In rough weather you start at a crouch and you may end up shuffling along on your bottom. In this way, as well as being clipped on, you have a much lower centre of gravity, are more stable and are wedged between the side rails and the side of the coachroof.

You will often come across seemingly experienced crew either not wearing harnesses, or wearing them but then not clipping the safety line on. That is up to them. They are taking a risk based on a belief in their own ability to stay on board just using their hands, possibly because they see it as being a macho thing to do, more likely because they are fed up with tripping over the safety line, getting it tangled around their feet, around the shrouds, getting to the end of the safety line and finding they can't quite reach whatever fitting or rope they are after; and in their frustration, they simply stop clipping on. Without clipping on they can nip out of the cockpit, free off a sheet, and then nip back again in seconds; with a harness on, the job can easily take twice as long. They are taking a calculated risk. If their calculations prove wrong, then they may not be around to apologise later for putting the boat and everyone else at risk, in trying to rescue them. If it is the skipper, then he must think you are pretty good crew; if you see him doing just this, then it might be worth congratulating him on his expression of confidence in your ability to pick him up out of the water if he falls in.

It is important once the boat starts bouncing around to clip on in the cockpit; and to stay clipped on when descending the companionway steps to make your companions a cup of tea; and equally if not more important, to clip back on before coming up the steps again. As you climb the steps facing the back of the boat, you are at your most vulnerable just as you reach the top step. More than one crewmember has gone from the warmth and comfort of the cabin for an unexpected swim in a cold sea, by-passing the cockpit altogether.

A safety harness once adjusted to your size is your personal kit and you must be responsible for it, know where it is and not pinch anyone else's. It is as much an integral part of sailing as a woolly hat and wellington boots. You should wear it, clip on, get used to using it (and it is a pain at times) and use it whenever conditions dictate, without even thinking about it.

Safety below

Moving around down below presents its own problems, not the least being the effect it can have on your ability to withstand being seasick, but at least you are not going to fall off the boat. Here it is a matter of common sense that you hang on the *grab rails*, lengths of timber fitted to the roof or sides, and any secure fittings, not the oil lamps and possibly not the table either, sit down as soon as possible wedged in a comfortable position, and remain wary of being thrown from one side of the cabin to the other. If you want or need to lie down, then you will find that either *lee cloths*, *lee boards* or *bunk boards* are available to keep you secure in your bunk. They simply form another side to the bunk to prevent you from falling out.

If you are working at the galley, then you need another safety strap, called inelegantly a *bum strap*, to secure you beside the cooker. This time the strap does help you keep your balance because you can lean back against it. The cooker has to be of a type suited to use at sea and not just in harbour, which means it has to rock backwards and forwards on hinges called *gimbals*; any pan or kettle must be clamped to the top of the cooker and extreme care must be exercised when pouring hot liquids. It is safest to wedge together all the required cups or mugs in the sink and then fill them up without holding them. Never end up with a kettle in one hand and a cup in the other; that is the surest way known, short of plunging your hand inside the kettle when it boils, of getting scalded.

Beware also pans containing hot liquids, especially thick liquids such as soup, tipping towards you. When working at the galley you should at least be wearing thick trousers, not shorts, preferably your oilskin trousers, and they must not be tucked into your boots. Tucked in, they direct the liquid straight down to your feet where it gets trapped by your boots, and you immediately have a serious medical problem that can only be dealt with properly on shore. The bum strap prevents you from falling backwards away from the cooker but you also need a crash bar in front of the stove to prevent you being thrown onto the front of the cooker. Incidentally, the cook's job is regarded as the worst on a small yacht.

Lifejackets

Many people new to sailing assume that you should wear lifejackets all the time. In fact lifejackets are worn very infrequently as they come into the category of survival equipment rather than safety. A safety harness is vital to stop you falling in the water. If you fall in, then a lifejacket would certainly be a handy piece of kit to have, but the priority is not to fall in. Lifejackets come in many different designs but the basic requirement is that a jacket should support the wearer in the water and result in the casualty floating face up. They are worn over the head and chest, held on with a waist band and preferably a crotch strap (unfortunately rare) to prevent the jacket riding up and strangling the wearer, have reflective tape stuck on them and some means of summoning help such as a whistle. The more advanced designs may have built in flashing lights, a radio alarm signal which triggers off an alarm on the boat, and some even have a sort of homing beacon to enable the yacht to find you.

A basic problem with lifejackets is that to provide sufficient buoyancy they need to be bulky, and trying to work a yacht whilst wearing a fully inflated lifejacket would be dangerous; the bulk of the jacket would severely restrict your ability to manoeuvre. To get over this problem the lifejacket can be worn deflated, and then inflated only when in the water, either orally by blowing into a valve, or semi-automatically by a gas canister which you set off by pulling a toggle, or totally automatically on contact with sea water. There are all sorts of arguments for and against different levels of technology being incorporated into lifejackets. On a cruising yacht they are worn in extreme sea conditions; when there is imminent danger of the ship sinking due to an accident, or of hitting an object and then sinking; in fog; and should be, and very rarely are, worn when going ashore by dinghy.

If you are a non-swimmer going on board for the first time, you should seriously consider wearing one of the deflated type, at least until you have got your sea legs and can move around the boat comfortably. The skipper may well ask you to, and if you refuse, he has a difficult decision to make.

All crew wear them in fog, even crew down below, as if you hit something, or something very large hits you, you are immediately in a survival not safety situation.

Survival suits

If your skipper kits you out in one of these, ask him where he is heading. It may be time to change boats. A survival suit is just that, a complete covering from head to foot that enables you to survive for lengthy periods of time in extremely cold conditions, both on board and in the water. It insulates you from the cold as well as providing buoyancy. They are only likely to become more commonly used when their prices drop.

Boat Safety

All crew are jointly responsible for the safety of the boat, and consequently each other. After all, if the boat goes down you will all sink together, competent crew and skipper alike. Looking after the boat encompasses everything from the minor actions of tidying up loose ropes, pointing out to the skipper anything you think might be amiss but are not sure is wrong and keeping a good look out, even though you have not been asked to, through to being able quickly to deal with emergencies such as fire. It is no use saying later, 'Well I thought it strange us sailing under the front of the cross channel ferry like that but I didn't like to say anything', or 'Well I thought I could smell burning'. Real accidents, that is events that could not have been prevented from happening, are rare. Most incidents can be traced back to something simple like not checking the engine oil before setting off, not turning the gas off when finished cooking, not tying the anchor back on to the deck securely after leaving an anchorage, not having a good look round before leaving a marina berth. If you keep leaving the gas on, then it is not an accident if eventually the gas builds up under the floor of the cabin, in a space called the *bilges*, and when you strike a match the boat explodes. If you want to be safe, think safe and follow simple routines that reduce the risk of real accidents occurring.

Fire

Of all the dangers in sailing, this is the most grossly underestimated danger by skippers and crew alike. For some reason, perhaps simply because the boat is surrounded by water, the possibility of a fire on board is not perceived to be a serious threat. A common thread from the accounts of those that have experienced a fire on board a small yacht and survived, is the speed at which events take place. From the point when the fire starts to the time the situation is untenable can be two minutes or less.

Explosive fires These are gas and fuel based. The danger from fuel is obvious, the danger from gas less so. The problem with gas on a boat is that, as it is heavier than air, it sinks and in a boat it is trapped; it does not disperse through natural ventilation. The gas fills up all the spaces under the floor and then starts to creep up the sides of the cabin. There is little, if any, smell as the gas is at one layer and your nose is much higher, perhaps even out in the cockpit. It is too late once the match is struck.

With diesel fuel it is possible, but unusual, to get a sudden loss of fuel followed by an explosion, while with petrol it is an ever present danger.

Secret fires With a fuel fire, what is far more likely is that there will be a slow weeping of fuel from a loose pipe, the fuel sits in the bilges or on top of the engine, gets hot as the engine is run and then, well hidden from view, catches light. Electrical fires also often start in secret. On a boat the real danger is the connections between the engine and battery overheating and eventually setting something close by alight.

Careless fires Under this category come fires that are caused by such simple things as not extinguishing matches properly after lighting the cooker or oil lamps, filling up an empty but hot oil lamp with new fuel down below, if smoking is allowed below (very rare) not extinguishing the cigarette, smoking at the top of the companionway steps and not watching what happens to the match you have used when bent double trying to light the cigarette out of the wind, curious and bored children discovering this box of interesting looking fireworks complete with instructions on the outside of each of them on how to set them off (it has happened), putting something flammable, such as a glove or even a chart (a hanging offence), on the top of a hot cooker.

Prevention

Fuel When taking fuel on board, extinguish all naked flames, including cigarettes, mop up any spills and keep the accommodation closed off to prevent fumes going below. Check all fuel lines regularly. Check all spare fuel cans regularly as they can easily leak fuel into the bilges. Keep ancillary fuels such as petrol for the outboard, paraffin, meths or white spirit, out in the cockpit lockers, away from heat and check them. Note these are all jobs well within the remit of a competent crewmember.

Gas Gas can usually be turned on and off at three places: on the top of the bottle, near the cooker, and obviously at the front of the cooker. As the gas bottle is in an outside locker, it is usual only to turn the gas on and off here when coming on board or leaving the boat. The rest of the time the gas is handled with the two inside taps. The inside taps, both on the cooker and the connection to the cooker should be turned off every time the cooker has been used, even just to make a cup of tea. When coming on board after the boat has been left for say a week, the cabin should be ventilated and a manual, not electric, bilge pump operated to clear out any gas in the bilges. Any smell of gas must be investigated immediately.

A further safety measure that is currently advised is that as you finish cooking, leave the gas ring alight and turn off the cooker at the other inside tap, not the front of the cooker. This burns all the gas in the pipe between the tap and cooker (the danger with this approach is that you then forget to turn off the ring at the cooker). Again all these are competent crew matters. **Careless fires** Don't be careless.

We will look at tackling serious emergencies such as fires, man-overboard or abandoning ship later; there have been enough of the dire warnings for now. There is only one other matter that needs to be considered, something which has immense importance to personal safety and boat safety and is the most underrated danger of all as it is often treated as a joke, seasickness.

Seasickness

If you are feeling seasick, apart from the fact that you are no longer enjoying sailing and just want to get off the boat as soon as possible, your reactions slow down, your sense of balance is reduced, your awareness of danger is reduced, your willingness to do anything that involves moving, even turning your head to look round a sail to see if there is another boat, is strictly limited.

You are also prone to becoming hypothermic. You sit rigid in the cockpit and shiver with cold but there is no way you are going to go down below to get extra clothes. You want to go to the toilet but you are not going down below to be shut in a cupboard, not for anything. You may become argumentative and refuse help, and refuse to do what the skipper asks or suggests that you might do, to make things better for yourself. As far as you are concerned, you are dying a very slow and painful death and just want to be left in peace. It has been known in very extreme cases, for the individual to reason that if he steps off the boat, the problem will be resolved as it is the boat that is moving not the sea.

You may also become dehydrated as continuous vomiting drains the fluids from the body very quickly and there is an understandable reluctance to drink anything if all you do is bring it back up again. All in all, it seems a good idea to try and prevent yourself from succumbing to this most ancient of seafaring maladies and there are simple things that you can do to give yourself a better chance.

Prevention

Diet Be careful what you eat before going sailing; even what you eat the night before can affect you the next day. Diet is an entirely personal matter but it does seem to help most not to set off within minutes of having had a full cooked, or usually undercooked, fried breakfast. Eat little, and drink plenty of non-alcoholic beverages when first at sea. If you stop at an anchorage for lunch on your first day, remember you are sailing again in the afternoon. When you feel hungry, try nibbling biscuits, have peanuts and raisins, not chocolate bars. But keep drinking, even if you can only cope with bottled water. After a few days your body adjusts quite well and you may find that you have no problems for the rest of the holiday.

Seasickness tablets and patches There are quite a few different types of seasickness tablets on the market, and a slow absorption patch which can be purchased under prescription in the UK (available far more freely in

Europe). The patch is stuck on your neck behind your ear and feeds in a chemical over a prolonged period of time. The effectiveness of tablets and patches varies from person to person and each variety has side effects such as drowsiness or dryness in the mouth. If you decide to use them they should be taken before going sailing; it is a bit too late once you start vomiting. It is a matter of personal choice and experimentation. They have transformed sailing for many people. Others prefer to be seasick and hope their system will recover quickly.

Seabands These are small wrist bands with a button with bumps on it. The bumps press against the inside of the wrist and work on the same principle as acupuncture. Again, some find these most effective, others not.

What to do if you feel sick

As soon as you start to feel unwell, tell the skipper. You may be put on the helm to steer, which does help. Keep looking at the horizon, not the boat or cockpit. Try and keep warm, particularly your head and don't be shy about asking others to get you a warm jacket or hat from down below. Try and join in the conversations on board and take your mind off the fear that you are going to make a fool of yourself. Seasickness has existed since man took to the water: it is a natural body reaction, a sign that you are a human being, and nothing to be ashamed about.

Once you start being sick you are of course embarrassed, you head to the back of the boat partly to vomit over the stern but partly to get out of everyone's view. You are now becoming a problem to the skipper because he knows, no doubt from his own experiences, that you are vulnerable. Although it may seem to be the worst possible thing in the world to contemplate, going below is certainly the safest thing to do. Different people react in different ways but for most of us, if we go below and immediately lie down, or wedge ourself in a corner and close our eyes, matters improve quite quickly. We may even drop off to sleep.

The skipper is happy because you are safe and warm and are no longer a problem. You are not happy, but should soon start to feel a lot better than you did. Even if you spend the rest of the day dozing below, that is not a problem.

Seasickness is not a joke, it is a real problem and it can so easily put people off sailing for life. Once conquered, there is a tremendous excitement to be had from sailing a boat in moderate winds with the spray flying, the boat tramping along, and you happy in the cockpit clutching a mug of tea and thinking you wouldn't want to be anywhere else in the world.

But at the moment the skipper wants you to look out for any vessels coming into Plymouth harbour.

12
BUOYAGE

At our breakfast briefing, the skipper has told us that once we have the anchor up we are going to motor-sail out of Plymouth Harbour entrance following the buoyed channel. Once clear of the headland, shown as Rame Head on the chart, we are going to steer west and run along the coast past Looe Island until we can see the black and white tower at Gribbon Head, and then follow the buoys into Fowey. Once in Fowey we are going to come alongside one of the visitors' pontoons if there is a space; if not we will pick up one of the trotted moorings.

He has explained that we are motor-sailing out of the harbour for three reasons: first, as the wind is blowing directly into the harbour entrance it would mean us tacking backwards and forwards across the route taken by commercial shipping into the harbour; second, he wants to charge up the ship's batteries which are charged by running the engine; third, he wants to check before he goes out to sea that the engine is running properly. And he has explained that the reason we are going to put the main up at the same time as running the engine is that with the main hoisted it helps to stop the boat rocking from side to side so much; it acts as a stabiliser.

Getting Under Way

As it happens, today the boat is lying at anchor with the bow pointing into the wind which means we can hoist the main whilst still at anchor and in the shelter of the anchorage. All we then have to do is very gently motor forward pulling in the anchor chain until the chain goes vertically down into the water. Now comes the difficult bit, pulling up the anchor. It helps to have gloves on (you can get cheap yellow plastic coated gloves from the chandlers that are ideal for this) and you must have your feet protected with wellies or sailing shoes. You bend at the knees, crouch down and grab the anchor chain with both hands, and lean back and stand up at the same time. You never pull with your back bent. It helps if two people can do this together. Nine times out of ten the anchor breaks free from the bottom.

Even after the anchor has parted company with the sea-bed, the pull on your arms and back remains very high as you still have the weight of the anchor, and all the chain dangling down in the water, to support. Take your time. You take the length of chain which you have pulled up, round the foredeck cleat or Samson post and this takes a lot of the strain. If necessary cleat the chain off. Repeat the same process of bending down at the knees, grabbing the chain, leaning back, and cleating off. The weight gradually

111

reduces as you pull in more chain, until the anchor itself appears at the surface of the water. Do not be surprised to find the anchor covered in black glutinous mud, full of hopping marine life. It should also come as no surprise that as competent crew it is your job to clean the anchor (another reason for wearing wellies). Once cleaned with a stiff brush and buckets of water the anchor is stowed away.

The main is up, a bit quicker today, the engine is happily chugging away, and it is time for us to find our way out of the harbour. To do this our skipper has to be able to read the chart, understand what all the buoys mean, know the marine equivalent of the highway code called the *Collision Regulations* (an unfortunate abbreviation of their full title but used by everyone), and also to have looked up any special local harbour regulations concerning the movement of ships in this particular harbour. As competent crew it is our job to help him as much as we can by keeping a good lookout for all craft of any variety, jet skis to aircraft carriers, and help spot buoys, beacons, lighthouses, and describe their characteristics, both in daylight and at night.

Buoys

Buoys are described by a combination of terms; their shape, their colour, any lights they may display (not all buoys are lit), and any sounds they might make (other than clang if you hit them). Looked at in diagrams the system is logical, and easy to follow – at sea things become less clear. The basic shapes used are described as *Cans*, *Cones*, *IALA* or *Cardinal*, *Round*, and finally *Pillar* or *Spar*. The colours they are painted are red, green, yellow, yellow and black, red and black, and red and white. The lights they display are white, red and green and different buoys have different ways of showing these lights. There are two basic systems followed when laying buoys, the *Lateral* system and the *Cardinal*. The systems are shown in colour on the inside of the front cover of this book and I would suggest you look at them carefully first to get an idea of what is coming next.

Lateral Marks

As the name suggests these mark the edges of a channel. The red can shapes are to the left, the green cone shapes are to the right, as you enter a harbour or go up a river. (See inside of front cover.) They are described as being laid from seawards. The can shapes may be bright red and large, or almost black and small, and the green cones similarly may be bright green or impossible to see; both may or may not have additional smaller can or cone shapes on poles on top of them (called *top marks*). In the upper reaches of smaller estuaries the can may just be a tin can on the top of a pole, if that; there may just be wooden sticks or *withies* with no marks on them. Instead of proper can and cone shapes, even quite large lateral marks may have their shape made up in a sort of silhouette form with fins sticking out from a central pole. The important two points to remember are red cans to the left, green cones to the right, when coming in from the sea. Spot the first problem? What if you are leaving harbour?

If the buoys are lit, then surprise surprise, red buoys have red lights, green buoys green lights, and these lights flash on and off in the way stated on the chart, and not according to one universal sequence.

Cardinal or IALA Marks

The principle here is that the buoy, or combination of buoys, shows the safe way round a danger; and they do this by reference to the *cardinal marks* of the compass, ie north, south, east and west. (See inside back cover.) These buoys have a distinctive shape being tall pointed towers, they are painted yellow and black and have special top marks and distinctive lights. Look at the diagram and start with the north cardinal mark. First note the two solid triangles or arrows pointing upwards; the tower underneath is painted yellow and black with the black towards the top. Now look at the south cardinal mark. The two black triangles point downwards and the black stripe is now at the bottom. Now for the difficult ones. Look at the east cardinal and start with the triangles. Note one points up, the other down; and there are two black stripes, one at the top of the tower, one at the bottom, with a yellow band in between. The points and the black stripes go together. Look at the triangles on the west cardinal and you can see the same pattern being followed, the points of the triangles point towards each other and so the black stripe is in the middle of the tower with yellow at the top and bottom. North and south are easy to remember but east and west take time. The top marks on the east mark look rather like an E; the top marks on the west look like a W on its side.

The lights are very distinctive: they are always white and they follow the same sequence as a clock, with the east mark having three flashes, the south six, the west nine and the top continuous.

Looked at on the diagram, given that a north mark indicates that the safe water is to the north, it is obvious which way to go round the buoy. But remember at sea you could be approaching this buoy from any direction, including from the south and although the diagram indicates that the danger is marked on all sides, in practice there might be only one buoy. You also need to know which way north is: remember the earlier section on the importance of being able to use a ship's compass.

There are some other standard buoys used in addition to these lateral and cardinal buoys.

Isolated Danger Buoys

Sometimes a buoy is put more or less on top of a danger but there is safe water all round the obstruction. In this case you can pass any side of the obstruction, just don't get too close.The colours are black and red horizontal stripes and the top marks are two balls, not triangles. Again the light used is white but it flashes twice, then there is a pause and it flashes twice again, and so on; note in particular that at sea there is no fixed association of red equals danger or green equals safe.

Safe Water Marks

A most welcome sight is a red and white striped buoy, (see inside front cover) which may be round or tower shaped or even simply a pole, which tells you there are no dangers near it. The top mark is one red ball. Why have such a buoy, if there are no dangers? Well it is usually laid some way out to sea off a harbour entrance and tells you not only that you are in safe water, but that the harbour is nearby. Quite often the directions on how to get into a harbour start with 'approaching the safewater mark you then turn to.....'.

Again it has a white light, but the characteristics of each buoy have to be looked up on the chart or in the almanac.

Special Marks

These can be any of the shapes already mentioned, can, cone, pillar or tower, but they all share three characteristics: they are painted yellow; if lit, they have a yellow light; and if they have a top mark it is in the shape of an ×. These buoys are used to convey additional information, such as demarcating an area for water skiing, or one for swimming, or even for marking shipping lanes. You have to look at the chart to find out what they mean; you cannot tell what they are indicating just by looking at them.

Light Characteristics

Reference has been made to flashing lights and sectored lights and coloured lights. We unfortunately now run into a language problem as the terms used to describe lights, and the symbols shown on charts and in almanacs smack of early Greek again. But it is of interest to us, and of considerable help to the skipper, if we can master the basic patterns.

The basic patterns are quite logical. A light can only be on or off but it can be turned on and off at different speeds, and stay on or off for different lengths of time. It is by mixing these options up that a whole range of different light signals can be made. We will stick to the more obvious and common varieties and leave the skipper to look up the others. Look at the diagram on page 117 and try and relate it to the text. The abbreviations in brackets are the codes used to describe the light signals on the charts and in the almanacs.

Types of Flashing Light
Very Quick Flashing (V Qk Fl) In this case the light simply flashes on and off about ten times every five seconds.
Quick Flashing (Q Fl) Now the time is down to about once on and off a second.
Long Flash (L Fl) Now the light may be on for three seconds.

Cardinal Marks
If we relate these three characteristics to our IALA buoys we get the following patterns:
North Continuous flashing, quick or very quick.
East Three very quick flashes, pause for just under five seconds then very quick three again, over and over, the same pattern every five seconds [V Qk Fl(3)5s]; alternatively it might be three quick flashes, the pattern repeated every ten seconds [Qk Fl(3)10s].
South Six very quick flashes, followed immediately by a long flash (taking up about five seconds in all), a pause for about five seconds, then the pattern repeated, over and over every ten seconds [V Qk Fl(6)+L Fl.10s]; alternatively six quick flashes plus one long flash every fifteen seconds [Qk Fl(6)=L Fl.15s].
West Nine very quick flashes, a dark pause of about five seconds, then nine very quick flashes [V Qk Fl(9)10s] or nine quick flashes, a pause for about ten seconds, then the pattern repeated [Qk Fl (9)15s].

Intervals and Colours
So far, so good; now come the two difficult terms to remember, *isophase* and *occulting*:
Isophase (Iso) Now the light flashes on for a short period and then off for the same period, then on for the same period and off again and so on. In other words the periods of light and dark are equal. On two seconds, off two seconds, on two seconds etc.
Occulting (Occ) Instead of the periods of light and dark being the same, the light stays on for a period, goes off for a much shorter period, and then comes on again, almost as though it was blinking or winking at you.
    Another two terms you need to know, but may find much easier to comprehend, are *fixed* and *alternating*.
Fixed (F) Obviously, the light stays on.
Alternating (Alt) Now we have two colours coming on and off, white then red then white then red, and so on.
    It sounds horrendous but at sea you can pick up the IALA buoys reasonably well, and also the coloured lights both fixed and flashing ones (unless you are colour blind, or less colour sensitive to certain colours which is a major problem). It is invaluable to the skipper to have crew that can recognise these basic patterns.

Buoyage in Practice

Although in theory the system is straightforward enough, at sea we have to contend with certain practical problems:

1 The lateral and cardinal systems are used together. A shipping lane, even outside a harbour, may be marked out using lateral buoys and in these circumstances the buoys are laid following the direction of the tides around the UK (shown on the chart with a broad arrow). Once in harbour, cardinal marks may be used with lateral marks in no obvious sequence; it is common for cardinal marks to be used to indicate a turning point in a channel marked by lateral marks.

2 It is very difficult even in flat seas to work out whether you are looking at a cone or a can, or what type of IALA buoy it is, until close to them, because the colours and shapes don't register, especially on dull days; and the top marks may be obscured or confused by other ironmongery on the top of the buoys, such as radar reflectors. It is very common to approach a buoy straining your eyes to work out what on earth the top mark is, only for the top mark to fly off and continue fishing now its wings are dry. Once the waves start rocking the buoys around and you start going up and down as well, the problems become acute. Hence the need for all on board to keep a good look out and to be able to describe to the skipper what sort of buoy they think they are looking at.

3 It is difficult at night to work out some of the light characteristics of the buoys. It is usually easy to distinguish the difference between red, white and green lights, but not so easy to work out what the light signal is that is being emitted, and where the buoy is relative to other buoys and the coast. If looking directly in from seaward towards a busy commercial port, then it takes a lot of patience and skill to pick out the lights of the buoys from the often much brighter lights on shore, even car brake lights.

Fortunately, buoys are not the only assistance available to help us find our way about at sea.

Other Visual Aids

Lighthouses We tend to think of them as white towers standing on rocks out at sea, like the Eddystone Light off Plymouth, but they are found on harbour walls, on breakwaters, on cliff tops, at the bottom of cliffs and on headlands. They provide visual reference points both during the day and at night (remember the business of taking bearings using the hand-bearing compass). How far away they can be seen depends on the height of the tower and the strength of the light, information given on the charts and in the almanacs. Each lighthouse may show different light characteristics and these have to be looked up. Lighthouses often make use of what are called

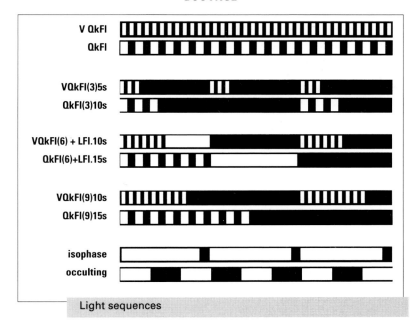

Light sequences

sectored lights, which are lights that can only be seen from certain directions. When approaching a harbour in the correct direction, if the light colour stays white, you are safe; if the colour turns to red or green, then you need to alter course as you are now *standing-in* (heading towards) danger (see diagram).

Lightships and Lanbys

Lightships are not common now, since most have been, or are in the course of being, replaced by Large Automated Navigational Beacons (hence Lanby). These are in effect floating lighthouses. The towers displaying the lights obviously cannot be so tall as a lighthouse but they are still effective. The light signal of a Lanby tends to be a distinctive brilliant white light, quite unlike a lighthouse. The advantages of a lanby over lightships and towers are that they are cheaper and they are unmanned. Again the actual signal has to be looked up.

Beacons or Towers

It is common to find unlit beacons on the tops of hills, especially near entrances to harbours or on headlands. Usually built many years ago as a navigational aid for local commercial shipping, they are an extremely useful aid to yachtsmen. It is surprising how difficult it is to work out where you

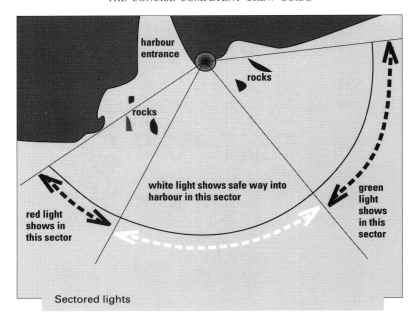

Sectored lights

are, when running along a rocky coast, with small headland after headland. You cannot relate what you see to what is on the chart. A beacon resolves any confusion. On an almost flat and featureless coastline, such as parts of the East Coast, any visual landmark is a god-send.

Leading Marks

To help you enter a harbour, marks are often put on the shore to lead you safely past hidden dangers, such as rocks, wrecks and sandbars. They are the ultimate in accurate position fixing. Look at the diagram on the previous page to see how they work. Two objects are placed one behind the other so that if you line them up you must be on the safe approach. The marks can be all sorts of shapes, some are lit, some are on the shore, others may have one of the marks in the water. They are shown on the chart, described in the almanac and are priceless. Once on the line you are safe.

It is common to have a whole series of such marks that first lead you into a harbour and then take you step by step up to a marina or safe anchorage. The marks used may not be navigational ones; the pilotage instructions might say 'keep the church tower in line with the electricity pylon until you can clearly see the white house, then turn to port bringing the white house on the foreshore in line with the conspicuous hotel on the hill behind'.

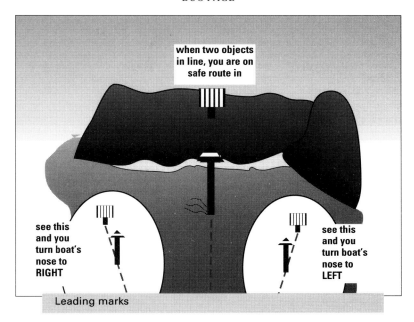

Leading marks

Disturbed Water

This requires skilled interpretation but it is still something to look out for and tell the skipper, especially when rounding a headland or approaching a harbour. If one patch of the sea is noticeably rougher than the sea around, perhaps with breaking waves or at least white crests, this can, (but not always), mark a shallow patch. It may simply mean that two different currents are meeting and mixing, say the water flowing out of a river and the tide flowing along the coast. In a harbour entrance it may mean either of these or both, but if the skipper is told he can then make his decision whether to proceed or alter course.

Sound Signals

Apart from visual aids there are sound signals, particularly signals made in fog. How many films have you seen with the mist whirling around and the eerie atmosphere turned up a notch with the sound of a booming fog signal. If you were disturbed by the film, in real life you may be reduced to a catatonic state, especially if you have sailed too close to the lighthouse or lanby and they have just turned on the noise. Some buoys have devices on them that make noises, sort of whistling and groaning noises (honestly, I am not joking) and by concentrating hard you can place their position very approximately just by listening. To be sure of their, and consequently your, position you have to sail in a direction such that the noise starts to get louder.

It is in fog that the immense value of electronic navigation systems is fully appreciated, as for obvious reasons you cannot see buoys and lighthouses, and sound signals give only an approximate position.

Smell

Again this is not a joke, but a serious point and one to store away at the back of the brain, as it is possible to locate oneself by a distinctive smell. If you are groping your way along the coast in fog, anything that can help the skipper fix your position must be considered of use. Sailing past an industrial town with the wind blowing off shore, you notice when you suddenly sail into an acrid smell. The direction of the wind gives you the position line pointing towards the town, and then the skipper has at least an approximate idea of where you are along the coast. This one piece of information may give the skipper just the chance he needs to start building up a picture of where you are, and hence get you home safely.

Westward Ho!

Fortunately, on our passage from Plymouth to Fowey we do not run into fog or need sound signals, but we see lighthouses, IALA and lateral buoys, and beacons. The beacon located on Gribbon Head the headland beyond Fowey Harbour, shows us we are getting near the harbour entrance which is completely hidden from us as we progress a few miles off shore sailing on a delightful beam reach in the southerly winds. The instructions from our *West Country Cruising Guide,* give us the information we need to approach the harbour safely and then enter it; the photographs prove particularly useful.

The skipper sails into the harbour but decides once inside, just as we are enjoying being waterborne tourists, looking round at the new scenery and taking it all in, that it is time to put the engine on, drop the sails, get the fenders out, get the warps out, and look for the visitor's pontoons.

Work, work, work – and this is supposed to be a holiday. Still the weather has been fine all day, despite the skipper muttering about getting depressed later in the week.

13
WEATHER

Our skipper shares the trait of all sailors: even when far inland they are obsessed by the weather, what it is doing now, what it might be doing tomorrow, in a few days' time, even next week. Sailing follows the dictates of the weather. We can only do what the weather will let us, and the weather may well prevent us from sailing at all. It dictates how fast we go, how comfortable the journey is going to be, and where we are going to end up. So all in all it seems like a good idea to be well informed about what the weather is doing now, and what it is likely to do in the future. It also helps to have a clearer understanding of what weather is, and the forces that drive it.

Our language is full of weather terms, and not just those that describe physical conditions such as rain, wind, sleet, snow, but ones which convey moods, a quiet spell, threatening, a louring sky. When at sea, weather terminology has precise meanings, ones which everyone can follow and know what to expect. There are terms to describe the strength and direction of the wind, visibility, the overall weather patterns, how quickly or slowly changes are to take place and when they are expected to take place, eg 'soon' has a precise, not general, meaning. We need to know what some of this terminology means in order to make best use of the vast amount of information freely available to us, every day, about the weather. We do not need to be expert weather forecasters ourselves, which is just as well – forecasting the weather is not an easy task as the Meteorological Office will readily confirm, even with highly skilled staff and one of the largest computers in Europe.

Weather Systems – Highs and Lows

Every sailing trip has its highs and lows but in this case we are talking about the two basic weather patterns that we experience, high pressure systems and low pressure systems. The term pressure relates to barometric pressure; but before you switch off completely this is not about to turn into a physics text book. Air actually weighs something; so think of high pressure as dense heavy air coming downwards and low pressure as lighter air going upwards.

High pressure system When the forecaster talks of a *high* pressure system sitting over southern England for the next few days, what is meant is that air is descending slowly towards the ground from much higher up in the atmosphere. 'So what?' you might say. For us sailors this means fine weather, few clouds, a possibility of strong winds (but gales are unlikely); more likely there may be little, or no wind at all, if the system becomes *established*, ie stuck. Also of major interest is the wind direction because wind flows round a high pressure system in a clockwise fashion (see diagram on page 124).

Low pressure system or depression Imagine you are having a bath, and then you pull the plug out. The water swirls round and round and tries to fill the hole up where the plug was, but instead, of course, disappears down the pipe. A low pressure system has at its centre a 'hole' which instead of going downwards actually goes upwards, a hole of low pressure or light air. All the air round about rushes towards it and tries to fill up the hole and the bigger the hole, the bigger the rush. A depression is therefore associated with strong winds. Depressions have other unwelcome characteristics too, such as rain, poor visibility and wind directions that can change rapidly when their weather fronts go through.

Weather Fronts

Think of a depression now as a cake, with a piece cut out (see diagram on page 124). Where the two cuts have been made are the places where the weather fronts are. The first weather front is called a warm front, and as this approaches the clouds get lower, it rains, it gets misty and the winds start to change from east through to south. Once the warm front goes past you enter the warm sector, which unfortunately does not mean everything gets better, it is still pretty miserable, with drizzle, low cloud and perhaps poor visibility; the wind becomes very changeable but the overall direction is south west. As we approach the other cut in the cake, we hit the cold front and there is a very rapid change in the weather. The wind goes round to the north west and picks up in strength and can be very gusty. Visibility is suddenly crystal clear, with bright blue skies between huge anvil shaped thunder clouds. Conditions under these clouds can be exceedingly unpleasant with violent gusts of winds and torrential rain. And cold it most certainly is, as the wind is coming from the north west.

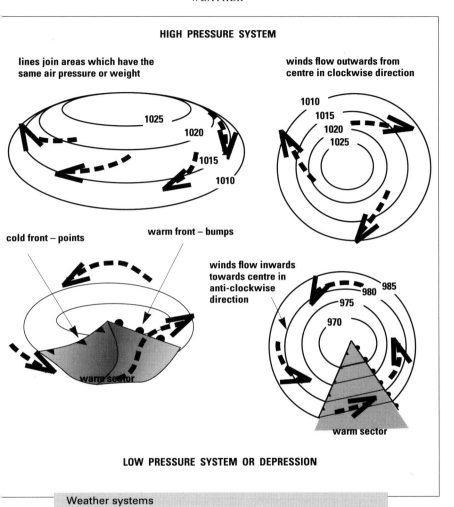

HIGH PRESSURE SYSTEM

lines join areas which have the
same air pressure or weight

winds flow outwards from
centre in clockwise direction

1025
1020
1015
1010

1010
1015
1020
1025

cold front – points

warm front – bumps

winds flow inwards
towards centre in
anti-clockwise
direction

985
980
975
970

warm sector

warm sector

LOW PRESSURE SYSTEM OR DEPRESSION

Weather systems

Measurement of Highs and Lows

This is done by an instrument which measures the weight of the air, a
barometer. Practically all boats have them; they look like clocks, and they
comprise a dial with an arrow that indicates the current barometric pressure. A summer high pressure system may typically have a barometric
pressure of 1025mb (millibars), the higher the number the stronger the

high, and therefore the less likely it is to change or move away quickly. Highs in these circumstances are described as being *stable*.

Low Pressure systems are inherently unstable and can move rapidly. An average low pressure system is going to be around the 990mb figure, but when lows are described as *intense*, or *deepening*, or *moving very rapidly*, then watch out. Storms are just around the corner. The barometric reading then will drop to somewhere in the 970-975mb range or even less.

The difference in pressure readings, and the fact that as a low pressure approaches the barometer readings start to fall, is why barometric figures are given out in shipping forecasts, and why the skipper wants the readings on our ship's barometer put down in the log book at hourly intervals. Any rapid or even constant change downwards will alert the skipper to the fact that something is on the move and it might not be a bad idea to start thinking of heading for a sheltered harbour.

Weather Forecasts

Our skipper listened to the VHF radio on board to get the latest weather information from the Coastguards. This is just one of an extraordinary number of sources of weather information open to us, most of them free. The almanacs list most sources of marine weather information, and how they are *promulgated* (sent out). To these can be added all the weather forecasts on television and in the newspapers. Once on board our basic sources of information are:
1 broadcasts on BBC Radio and local commercial radio stations;
2 broadcasts on VHF radio;
3 radio facsimile (fax) transmissions.
We can use the VHF to get additional information available through the telephone network including:
1 Marinecall, a pre-recorded information service;
2 direct from the Met Office.

Not all the forecasts are the same, some are far more detailed than others, but they all use the same language, so we need to learn at least the basic terminology. We have already made a head start with highs and lows and weather fronts and barometric pressure. All we need add now are the terms describing wind, visibility, the passage of time and sea state.

The Beaufort Scale

Imagine you are in charge of a huge naval fleet and you want each ship to record the wind speed every day in their logs, only the ships don't have wind speed indicators. Rear-Admiral Sir Francis Beaufort came up with the answer in 1895 when he devised a system of numbers that related wind speed to the effect it had on the amount of sail a Man-of-War could carry. The Beaufort system was adopted by the navy and spread outwards, and is so good that it is still the system used to describe wind speeds, although the numbers of his system can now be related to actual wind speeds in knots. The system has numbers that go from 0 to 17 but commonly only 0 to 12 are used. The beauty of the system is that it enables wind speed to be correlated with the conditions the wind causes at sea, particularly wave action. The whole table is given in the diagram opposite. The numbers down the left hand column are described as wind *force*, force three, force four etc. So each and every forecast talks of wind speeds in these terms.

For small boat sailors like ourselves a broadcast of a *Strong Wind Warning* equates with a Strong Breeze which is a force 6, sometimes colloquially referred to as a Yachtsman's gale to distinguish it from a true gale, force 8. It is common to have forecasts which combine several numbers, eg force 3 to 4, occasionally 5 later in east. You soon get tuned in to what a force 3 means when at sea, excellent sailing; force 4 and things are getting a little boisterous; force 6 and it is 'why am I out here and not in harbour, never again'.

Wind Direction

This causes us little problem as the points of the compass are used, north, south, east and west, and the combinations, such as south-west, north-north-east, also can be worked out without too much effort. The main point to remember is that if the wind is a south-westerly, it is coming from the south-west, not going towards it, a northerly wind is approaching us from the north and so on. Two terms you will hear are *backing* and *veering*. If the wind is coming from the south and then moves round to east, it is moving anticlockwise and this is called backing; if the wind goes from south to west, it is said to be veering.

Visibility

The one word you do not want to hear in a weather forecast is fog; this is far more feared than strong winds. Electronic navigation systems, including radar, have tamed some of its terror but by no means all. It is often assumed that fog is always associated with calm seas and little wind; this is not the case at sea where you can easily have fog with wind. Visibility can also be reduced to near fog level in heavy rain, not a cheerful experience anywhere close to land.

No	Knots	Described	Deep Sea Criterion
0	‹ 1	Calm	Sea like a mirror.
1	1-3	Light breeze	Ripples with the appearance of scales are formed but without foam crests.
2	4-6	Light breeze	Small wavelets, still short but more pronounced. Crests have a glassy appearance.
3	7-10	Gentle breeze	Large wavelets. Crests begin to break. Foam of glassy appearance. Perhaps scattered white horses.
4	11-16	Mod. breeze	Small waves, becoming longer: fairly frequent horses.
5	17-21	Fresh breeze	Moderate waves, taking a more pronounced long form; many white horses are formed. (Chance of some spray).
6	22-27	Strong breeze	Large waves begin to form, the white foam crests are more extensive everywhere. (Probably some spray).
7	28-33	Near gale	Sea heaps up and white foam from breaking waves begins to be blown in streaks along the direction of the wind.
8	34-40	Gale	Moderately high waves of greater length; edges of crests begin to break in to spindrift. The foam is blown in well-marked streaks along the direction of the wind.
9	41-47	Strong gale	High waves. Dense streaks of foam along the direction of the wind. Crests of waves begin to topple, tumble and roll over. Spray may affect visibility.
10	48-55	Storm	Very high waves with long overhanging crests. The resulting foam in great patches is blown in dense white streaks along the direction of the wind. On the whole the surface of the sea takes a white appearance. The tumbling of the sea becomes heavy and shocklike. Visibility affected.
11	56-63	Violent storm	Exceptionally high waves. (Small and medium sized ships might be for a time lost to view behind the waves). The sea is completely covered with white long patches of foam lying along the direction of the wind. Everywhere the edges of the wave crests are blown into froth. Visibility affected.
12	64+	Hurricane	The air is filled with foam and spray. Sea completely white with driving spray; visibility very seriously affected.

Beaufort Scale

There are four basic terms used to describe visibility in shipping forecasts and they are:
Fog Less than 1,000 metres
Poor 1,000 metres to 2 nautical miles
Moderate 2 to 5 nautical miles
Good more than 5 nautical miles.
Sometimes when the visibility is markedly less than 1,000 metres further information may be given.

A distance of 1,000 metres may seem quite substantial, but not when you are at sea. And just because you are going slowly, it doesn't mean others are, particularly commercial shipping which has to meet strict timetables. A yacht travelling at 5 knots covers a mile every 12 minutes, a ferry doing 25 knots covers 6.25 miles in the same time. With visibility down to 2 miles, the ferry will be on you within 5 minutes of you seeing him. A useful indicator of distance is that when sitting in a cockpit of an average yacht, the sea horizon is about $2^1/_4$ miles away.

Time

Time is handled in forecasts by dividing the next twenty-four hours into three periods:
Imminent within 6 hours
Soon within 6 to 12 hours
Later 12 to 24 hours
So if you hear a forecast which says that force 6 winds are imminent, you have less than 6 hours to find shelter.

Other Weather Terms used

The forecast weather itself may be described, such as thundery showers, or actual weather described such as *precipitation* (rain) *in sight*.

The rate at which the barometer rises and falls is described in terms of *steady*, *falling* or *rising*, with other adjectives such as *quickly* and *slowly* used. If the barometer readings start to drop at a rate of more than 1mb an hour and this keeps up or accelerates to say 6mb over a 3 hour period then it is time for the mooring warps and a pint ashore.

The speed at which a depression moves is described on a scale that goes from *slowly*, 0-15 knots, to *very rapidly*, over 45 knots. Note that even a slow moving depression may well be moving towards you faster than you can sail out of the way.

Forecast Areas

The whole of the sea around the UK has been divided into about thirty notional areas (notional in the sense that they have no visible boundaries), using terms which make no sense to us as yet. It doesn't help to know it is blowing a gale in South Utsire and calm in Finisterre if you have no idea where either of these places is. A map of the sea area is given on page 130 and over time the names begin to drop into place, particularly the area you are sailing in. You can also see on the map big dots, with single letters beside them. These mark the locations where what is actually happening is recorded and the recordings made a short time before the forecast is given out are read out as part of the weather forecast; they are invaluable as they are the truth, not a forecast which may be wrong. You soon get to know the one nearest you and to listen out for it.

The full shipping broadcast lasts five minutes and is broadcast four times a day at set times (currently 0033,0555,1355 and 1750) by the BBC. It is read out at normal speed and is impossible to take down without a lot of practice. It starts with the overall *synopsis* or picture of what is going on with the lows and highs, then goes round the country clockwise giving out information for each sea area. The broadcast ends with the reports from the weather coastal stations. Another broadcast is made twice a day, currently after the 0033 broadcast and at 0655, which is of particular interest to us and called the *Inshore Waters Forecast.*

Each individual shipping forecast area covers huge tracts of sea, and even these may be combined to form one bigger forecast area, such as 'Thames, Dover, Wight, Portland, Plymouth'. It is inconceivable that at the local level the weather conditions are going to be the same for such a large area, even though the general trend of the forecast may be correct. A separate forecast is given of the weather conditions it is thought likely will occur within twelve miles of the coast, hence the title; and incorporated within this forecast is detailed information about weather conditions actually experienced at a whole series of locations around the coast.

Yet our skipper listened to the VHF in the morning, not the BBC, to get his forecast and he had no trouble writing it down.

VHF Coastguard Weather Service

The Coastguards operate many excellent services for smallboat sailors but the weather forecast ranks pretty highly. They broadcast at four hourly intervals the synopsis for the country taken from the full shipping forecast, the inshore waters forecast for the local area they cover and they add current information about not only the weather but the sea state, whether the sea is calm or rough or has a moderate swell and so on; and best of

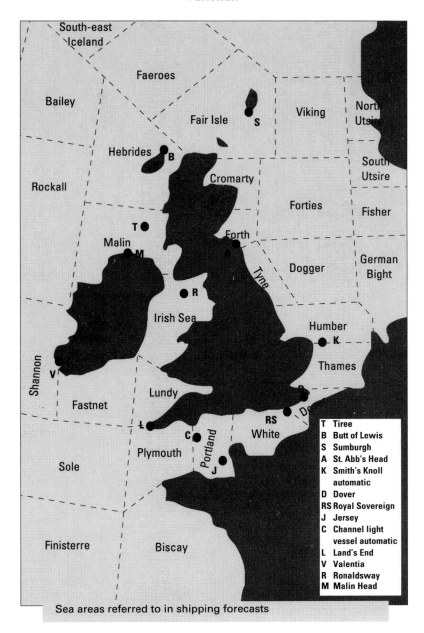

Sea areas referred to in shipping forecasts

all they do it very slowly and repeat it as they go along.

Why our skipper was muttering about being depressed after listening to the VHF radio was that the forecast told him the high pressure system was moving slowly away to the east. Although no mention was made of a low pressure system moving in from the west, he knew that the most likely situation was that somewhere out in the Atlantic there was a low pressure system waiting to move in once the high shifted out of the way.

As competent crew we can help the skipper, first by being absolutely silent while the forecast is on; second, by listening to the forecast ourselves so that we can help fill in a gap if a pencil breaks at a vital moment; and third, by learning how to read a barometer – which takes one minute – and making relevant notes in the log. But at the moment the weather is fine.

14
ENGINES

After mooring up to the visitors' pontoon which is not beside the shore but out in the river, our skipper demonstrates another use of the VHF by calling up a water taxi to take us ashore. No need to pump up the dinghy this evening. And after a convivial evening ashore and a quiet night on the pontoons, next morning the skipper listens to the forecast on the VHF and is still uncertain what is likely to happen later in the week. Over breakfast he mulls over the information that the wind is backing slightly to the south-east, ideal for going on to the next harbour he wants to visit, Falmouth, about twenty or so miles south-west, but the synopsis has for the first time referred to a slow moving low pressure system out in the Atlantic.

The normal ship routine of tidying up, washing up and getting the sails sorted out is well underway when the skipper decides to check the engine, something he has been meaning to do every day but has only done once before, just before we first left harbour.

The engine is buried under the cockpit floor but access to the front of the engine can be gained by removing the whole of the companionway steps. With a torch the skipper quickly checks over the engine for any obvious leaks of water, oil or fuel and then, just as in a car, he checks the oil level with a dipstick and, much to his surprise, we have very little left. He pulls up the panels in the floor to look inside the bilges and, sure enough, floating down there is a pool of oil.

Diesel Engines

It is unusual now to find a yacht with a petrol engine. Diesel engines have many advantages not the least being that the fuel is much safer as it does not catch light and explode so easily as petrol. Diesel engines do not require such complicated electronics as a petrol engine, and once started do not require electricity to keep running. The way a diesel engine works is very simple. The engine has cylinders with pistons inside them, just as with a car, and the pistons go up and down the cylinders. In a car engine as the piston goes up inside the cylinder, at exactly the right moment, the right amount of petrol is introduced, a spark is created by the spark plug, and the subsequent explosion of the petrol as it ignites and burns, pushes the piston back down again. This process is repeated at very high speed to produce the required power. Any failure in the electrical supply to the spark plug,

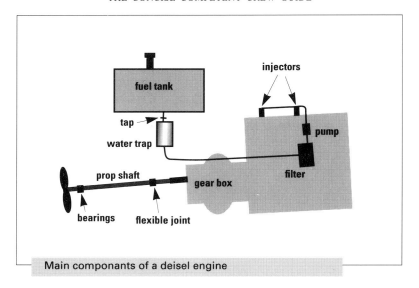

Main componants of a deisel engine

or if the timing of the spark is fractionally out, means the engine stops working.

With a diesel engine there is no spark plug. The piston goes further up inside the cylinder, compressing the air much more than in a petrol engine and so heating it up, a fine spray of diesel fuel is introduced through a fuel injector and, as a result of the compression, the explosion takes place, forcing the piston down again. The speed at which this system operates tends to be slower than with a petrol engine and you only have the one control to worry about, the fuel injector. The fuel injector itself is not a particularly complicated piece of machinery, though it is prone to becoming blocked by dirty fuel. The only reason you need electricity to start a diesel engine is to get the pistons going up and down inside the cylinders fast enough to start the process off; once started it should continue happily on without any further attention.

Some diesel engines have emergency starting handles should the battery fail, but unless the engine is very small the chances of being able to start an engine this way are remote. Which is why it is common to have two batteries on a yacht, one reserved just for starting the engine.

To stop a diesel engine you do not turn off the electricity supply as this has no effect on the engine, though it has a dramatic effect on certain of the electrical equipment attached. The engine runs an electrical charging system which keeps going even if the electrical supply side is turned off. All the electrical energy still being created by the engine has to go somewhere and there is a tendency for this energy to be converted to heat, easily detected by the smell of melting equipment, smoke and fumes. You stop the engine by pulling a cable in the cockpit which affects the fuel supply, and only when the engine has stopped rotating do you turn off the electrical circuits.

A diesel engine works in a pretty hostile environment: it is constantly being shaken up at sea, sucks in salty air all the time but worst of all, it is used only very spasmodically. It may sit idle for three weeks, everyone piles on board, the engine is started just to get the boat out of the marina, and before the oil is properly circulating and the engine warmed up, it is switched off again – only to be started and stopped again at the end of the day. It is no wonder there are problems and why about half the calls made by small craft for assistance from the Lifeboats are because of engine failure.

Clean Fuel

The system depends on clean fuel, and unfortunately it is all too easy for all sorts of rubbish to get into the fuel supply. It starts when fuel is taken on board and although a nuisance, as it slows down the process enormously, it is best if fuel taken on board is passed through a filter, even a crude wire gauze filter inside a fuel funnel helps, as this stops the larger bits of rust and debris getting into the tank. Between the fuel tank and the engine it is common to have two or three filters designed to remove any water that might have inadvertently got in the tank and any more bits of debris.

As competent crew little more is expected of us other than to be careful when taking on fuel. However it is worth asking the skipper to point out the filters as one day we may have to help in cleaning one out if the fuel supply gets blocked. As the engine sits in the marina all the sediment sinks to the bottom of the fuel tank. This does not cause an immediate problem when the engine is started as fuel is not usually drawn off from the very bottom of the tank. Once at sea, especially in rough conditions, the sediment starts to get churned up and mixed back with the fuel. If the engine then has to be started in an emergency, there may well be a problem before too long; so all in all it is a good idea to be fussy about fuel.

Checking the Oil

As with a car a diesel engine is lubricated with oil. And just as with a car the oil has to be kept topped up to the right level and changed at the correct time intervals; and somewhere in the system there will be an oil filter that has to be cleaned or replaced at regular intervals. As competent crew we should know where the dipstick is so that we can check the oil level; and it helps to know where the oil filter is as well. On some boats there are two dipsticks, one for the engine oil and another for the oil inside the gearbox; we should know where this one is and be able to check it as well.

Cooling the Engine

Again as with a car, the engine is cooled by water being pumped round, and at least at sea there is no shortage of water. Although not so sensitive as the fuel supply, obstructions in the water supply side can generate problems. With a seawater cooled engine, water is taken in under the boat through a seacock, pumped round and then sent out the back mixed with the exhaust gases from the engine.

As competent crew it is our job when the engine is started to check by leaning out over the back of the boat that water is in fact being pumped out. If not, the seacock has not been turned on; or there is a blockage in the inlet pipe; or the pump has broken. Some water pumps are pretty fragile efforts. Inside them is a plastic *impeller*, something with fins on which pumps the water round, and they break if anything comes in through the seacock, such as bits of seaweed. If the seacock is blocked on the outside of the hull, by say an over curious fish, then the only satisfactory way of unblocking it is to get into the water and poke around with a wire which is definitely a job for the skipper. I mean, there is such a thing as being too keen as crew.

Our skipper meanwhile has discovered the source of the problem, the oil filter is leaking. He has tightened it right up but it is still weeping, so he has decided to fit a new one. He had been meaning to get a spare for ages but had never got round to it so he will have to go and get one from the chandlers. Still, as crew we are not in the least perturbed as this means another trip ashore. We all fancy going in the dinghy this time to get a bit of exercise by rowing ashore, but the skipper advises that only three of us should go in the dinghy as the river is very busy and the wash from passing boats would make the journey unsafe for all five of us. He is going by water taxi anyway as he will be bringing back a full can of oil as well as a new filter. It is tactlessly pointed out by a more knowledgeable member of the crew that if only we had an outboard engine we could ferry everyone back and forwards to the shore but as far as the skipper is concerned arms were made for rowing, outboards made for trouble.

Outboard Engines

It is common to have a petrol driven outboard engine on a cruising yacht to help get ashore, especially as it is exceedingly difficult to row an inflatable dinghy in windy conditions, or fully laden with crew and stores. The engines usually run on a mixture of fuel and a little oil, the balance between the two varies from engine to engine. The smallest engines are designed to be portable and they simply clamp onto the back of the dinghy. They start by having the fuel turned on and by pulling on a long cord. If the inboard engine has a hard time, then the outboard engine is asked to do the impossible, usually on zero maintenance.

As competent crew we should be able to fit the engine on the dinghy, be able to start and stop the engine, either by closing the throttle (or accelerator) right down or by turning off the fuel, and fill it with fuel (just poured in the top, again through a filter funnel). The engines have their own tilting mechanism so that as we approach the shore, the engine can be tilted forward into the dinghy and that way the propeller is not damaged by hitting the ground. Although relatively small, they are still heavy and care has to be taken when lifting them in and out of the yacht in order to put them on or take them off the dinghy; it is best to tie the engine on to the yacht before moving it either way, in or out of the cockpit, as it does not float if dropped! They produce a considerable amount of power and care has to be taken when using them, especially near anyone actually in the water; and they also produce a great deal of noise, which is another reason why our skipper is so anti-outboards.

It takes most of the morning for the skipper to buy what he wants and fit the new filter and so he informs us that we will have lunch where we are and wait until the 1350 shipping forecast on the radio before he finally makes his mind up whether to risk going further west. The passage to Falmouth is straightforward and only about 20 odd miles, so even at a slow $3^1/_2$ knots we can get there and be tied up in under eight hours in the forecast light south-easterlies. Falmouth is a safe harbour in any weather so the skipper is not worried about the entrance; what is concerning him is the approaching low pressure system and the fifty mile passage back to Plymouth which we have to make to get the boat back by the end of the week.

While waiting for lunch, he decides after this morning's unpleasant surprise that he had better start running through some of the procedures for dealing with possible mishaps on board, just in case.

15
EMERGENCY PROCEDURES

The record of sailing as a safe sport is a good one, despite the fact that most skippers and crew tend to be a bit lackadaisical about safety. It is sometimes difficult to strike a balance between being prepared and kitted up for every likely possible emergency situation and sailing around in a state of apprehension waiting for disaster to strike, and adopting the opposite approach of 'it will never happen to me', because it just might.

It is an obvious truism that prevention is better than cure, and this is particularly the case when sailing, as the emergency services which we rely on as a matter of course on land, everything from the AA and RAC to the casualty department of our local hospital, are simply not available at sea.

It is no use ignoring the fact that accidents, whether preventable or not, do happen on board. And the best way of reducing the risk of such accidents turning into serious emergencies, is to have set procedures that everyone can follow immediately the problem occurs.

Coping with Fires

Any fire on board is a potentially lethal event and every possible precaution must be taken to stop one starting. This involves such simple things as being careful with gas, fuel, matches, oil lamps, electricity, cigarettes, pipes – absolutely anything that could start a fire. But let us suppose the unthinkable happens and a fire starts, how can we put it out safely? Fires need three ingredients to keep going, heat, oxygen and fuel and we need to tackle at least one, even better all three, to get the fire under control and then put it out.

Fire Extinguishers

A boat must carry sufficient extinguishers to put out a small fire quickly and stop it from spreading. It is unrealistic to assume that once it has a hold you will be able to get control back just using ordinary equipment. The types of extinguishers commonly found on yachts are the dry powder type, where the cylinder is colour coded blue, and Halon or BCF gas type colour coded green. The extinguishers themselves can present a hazard, particularly the halon or gas variety as they produce highly toxic fumes. Once a halon extinguisher is let off you must leave the area immediately and not come back until it has been well ventilated; so although commonly found on boats they are not ideal and are due to be banned in the near future anyway for other reasons. Both types operate by removing one of the ingredients of the fire, oxygen. Neither cool the fire down or stop more fuel being available.

Fire Blankets

It is essential to have one of these near the cooker, but not immediately above it or behind it as it may then be impossible to get to it. All that is required is to drape the blanket over the flames of whatever has caught light on top of the cooker. This again simply excludes oxygen, not fuel or heat.

Water

The boat is surrounded by an excellent fire fighting medium, which unlike the chemical or gas extinguishers, is of almost unlimited supply. Water is good at reducing heat and at temporarily cutting off oxygen, if used in sufficient quantities, and is not toxic. Unfortunately it causes other problems if put on an electrical or fuel fire. If the power is still on, it can help cause a minor explosion, and in any event will certainly wreck the electrical equipment; and if water us put on any fuel fire, then instead of putting the flames out, it may simply spread them, as the burning fuel will float on the surface of the water and be transported round the boat.

Emergency Procedures

All on board need to know how to deal with the situation immediately, although obviously the first thing to do is shout *fire on board!* and alert the skipper, and everyone else, to the problem. Fires down in the accommodation area are likely to start due to problems related to the engine, to cooking and to people being careless while smoking or lighting lamps.

Engine Fires

These can start unnoticed as the engine compartment is completely enclosed. The fire is most likely to start either when the engine is running, or has been running and has just been turned off so that the engine block is still very hot. The fire can be quietly getting underway without the engine stopping if it is running. The first signs may be a burning smell and fumes coming round the sides of the engine hatches and the most natural reaction of all is to go down below, pull off the inspection hatch at the front of the engine, which also most likely entails removing the companionway steps, to see what the problem is. This provides a smouldering fire with just the extra oxygen it needs and we now have a major problem. We have not only made the fire roar into life but also just cut off our quickest means of escape from down below, or worse still, our only means of escape on a small yacht if it does not have a large forehatch that we can climb out off. On many yachts it is common now to have a fire extinguisher strapped to the engine inspection hatch with a nozzle leading straight through inside the engine compartment. This means the extinguisher can be discharged safely without having to open the hatchway. On larger yachts this may even be done automatically via a heat and smoke sensor.

The foam is released covering everything inside, and when the extinguisher is empty, then is the time gently to open the inspection hatch a fraction to see what is going on. In the meantime, additional firefighting equipment can be brought to the scene, such as another portable extinguisher or buckets of water. Once the hatch is off the remains of the fire, if it is still smouldering, can be doused with the second extinguisher or with water splashed from the bucket. It is better to splash water rather than throw it over everything in sight.

Remember heat, fuel, oxygen; we have dealt with heat and oxygen but we need to shut off the fuel as well, which may be actual fuel from a broken fuel line. Underneath the fuel tank in the cockpit will be a tap; this gets turned off by anyone in the cockpit as soon as it is realised there is an engine fire. The engine is stopped, if still running, by pulling the stop cable and the electricity is turned off. All this must happen in an instant without the need for the skipper to give many, if any, instructions.

After the fire has been put out or at least brought under control, a careful inspection must be made to see what damage has been caused. Some of the plastic tubing attached to the sea water inlets used to provide the engine with water, or outlets to drain water from the bottom of the cockpit may have melted. If the seacocks are open then the fire will soon be permanently out, but you will not appreciate the good side to this, as you watch the boat sink.

A Galley Fire

This is easier to deal with, providing the fire is smothered immediately with the fireblanket so that the area above the cooker does not catch light. If it does, then the portable extinguisher must be used very quickly. As with the engine fire, once the shout goes up *galley on fire!*, anyone in the cockpit immediately turns off the tap on the gas bottle in the gas locker without waiting to be told. If the lining on the roof does catch light, the biggest danger is the person nearby being overcome with fumes and having bits of burning plastic drop on them. Step back, hold the extinguisher upright (otherwise it may not work properly) and direct the jet or nozzle at the flames nearest to you and spray the fire from front to back in a sweeping motion, pushing the fumes and flames away from you. This is also the best approach for dealing with any sort of fuel fire.

Accommodation Fire

Here the danger is that everyone will be overcome by fumes before anyone notices there is a problem, especially if it has been caused by someone being careless smoking in their bunk. It is a case of everyone out fast, and away from the fumes. If there is no actual fire then it may be possible to shut the hatches and reduce the oxygen supply, get a bucket of water handy, and then a quick dash below to splash water over the smouldering mattress and then out again. If the seat of the fire is inside a mattress simply spraying it with an extinguisher may bring only very temporary relief.

As competent crew we should know how the extinguishers operate – it is a bit late to start reading the instructions on their sides once the fire has started – where the taps are to turn off the gas, fuel, and water inlets and basically what to do in an emergency.

Fire threatens the safety of the whole ship and everyone on board. The next emergency may involve just one person, but it could be the skipper, man overboard.

Man Overboard

Fall off a boat at night and there is little chance of being found, no matter how hard the crew try. Fall off during daylight hours and you may have a chance, providing everyone left on board knows what to do, and does it quickly. After the experience with the engine our skipper has decided that before the passage down to Falmouth, he had better run through what he expects to happen in such an emergency and to have a quick practice at sea, just after leaving harbour.

There is no one procedure that everyone follows; in fact what the best method might be to recover someone overboard is the subject of many a heated argument at yacht club bars. Whatever procedure is adopted, the start is always the same, the shout goes up of *man overboard!* as soon as it is realised that someone is missing. If the person has been seen to go overboard, then three things have to happen. First, visual contact with the person in the water has to be maintained at all costs; second, the boat has to be brought back to the casualty as quickly as possible; and third, the casualty has to be physically attached to the boat. Once these have been achieved, the crew can then concentrate on giving artificial resuscitation if necessary and then getting the crewmember back on board.

In any sort of sea, not just rough seas, it is very difficult to see a bobbing head in the water. If the casualty is spotted going over the side then, providing it is done immediately, a life belt can be dropped in the water. This provides the person in the water with some buoyancy but also

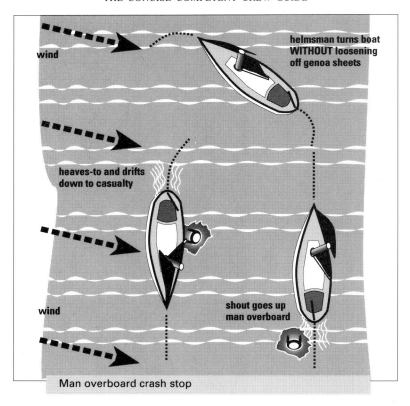

Man overboard crash stop

helps locate him as the lifebelt is luminous orange and has reflective strips attached to it. Better still, a *danbuoy* can be dropped with the lifebelt. A danbuoy is simply a pole with a flag on the top (sometimes it has a light as well) and is far easier to locate than a man's head. The crewmember swims directly towards the buoy where he will find the lifebelt attached to it by a floating line. For those on board the yacht, what they do now is determined by the skipper; if it is the skipper in the water, then it is a little late for him to run through what he wants them to do.

One procedure that is worth trying out in practice is to *crash stop* the boat. In our situation of sailing down the coast on a broad reach, if the helmsman immediately spins the boat round, either by tacking through the wind without touching the genoa sheets or by a controlled gybe, the boat is then hove-to and should be very close to the casualty, certainly within visual range. The boat may still creep forwards through the water but sail power can be quickly reduced simply by letting go the genoa halliard – the sail will fall down on the foredeck and not over the side – and letting the main sheet right out. A quick check to ensure that there are not any ropes dangling in the water and that the crewmember is not immediately under or near the stern, and then the engine can go on and the boat motored gently towards the crew member, being taken out of gear once nearby.

Once the casualty is alongside we may have to bring into play our expertise in knots and ropehandling in order to attach the crewmember to the boat and then hoist him or her, by whatever method the skipper suggests, back into the boat. It is most likely that the person will have to be winched back on board as brute force is rarely enough to lift a waterlogged crewmember.

Summoning Help

But what if, despite our efforts at fighting a fire we don't succeed, or we cannot find our crewmember in the water, or in the process of all of this someone is injured and needs assistance far beyond the resources of the skipper and the yacht's first aid kit (never usually a substantial affair and often pilfered to carry out running repairs on the boat), or the boat is damaged and cannot be sailed or motored. What next?

Well, we need help and we can summon this in a number of ways but the most reliable, if it is still operative after our emergency, is the VHF radio. Unlike the man overboard drill, there is a set procedure that must be followed by everyone, big ship and little alike.

VHF Radio Distress Calls

On the front of the VHF set is a dial or digital display showing the channel currently selected. There are lots of channels but each number has a prescribed use, some are reserved for communicating between ships, others ship to shore. The one used for sending a distress signal is Channel 16. There should be a button on the front of the set saying C16 which when pressed immediately cancels out the currently selected channel and locks the set on to 16. This channel is used by all ships for calling for help. It has other uses as well but once a May Day call goes out nobody can use C16 who is not directly involved in the distress situation.

To send out a distress signal, apart from the obvious need to check the set is switched on, you need to press another button on the front which should say *high* or *25W*. This means that the set is working at maximum power and the call will be heard by other ships and by the Coastguard, even though many miles away. To transmit a message you use a small plastic microphone with another button along one side, or occasionally you may find something that looks like a normal telephone handset. To transmit you have to push the button in, to receive you must let it go again. With the button pressed in no one can contact you. The message is said slowly and clearly, preferably in a slightly higher pitched voice than normal (not usually a problem under these circumstances) and always follows the same pattern:

MAYDAY, MAYDAY, MAYDAY,
This is YACHT TROUBLE, YACHT TROUBLE, YACHT TROUBLE
MAYDAY
YACHT TROUBLE

No one will answer just yet as you have not completed your message; you must continue following the next set sequence

I am in position ....

Now give the most accurate position possible using electronic navigation if fitted, otherwise something along the lines of 'I am 2 miles due southwest of Rame Head'. If you are not sure where you are, say so and give an approximate position, don't pretend.

(I am on fire/sinking/....or whatever applies)

It is important for your rescuers to know what the problem is so that they can take the most appropriate action.

Next comes vital additional information such as:

There are five adults on board, one severely burned, we have no liferaft but we do have distress flares.

When you have finished you say:

Over

and let go the button! From now on you will most likely be communicating with the Coastguards who are expert at dealing with emergencies and they will take you step by step through what they want you to do and when. They are in control. It is important to realise that although radio contact has been made, no rescue is imminent. You have to look after yourselves until rescue arrives.

If you face a problem which does not give rise to an immediate risk of loss of life, or loss of the yacht, but is still a problem you are unable to resolve, let us say the mast has gone over the side, you have cut it free but rope and sails are wrapped round the rudder and propeller so you can't start the engine or steer. You are not in any danger as yet but could be if you cannot sort things out within a couple of hours; then an alternative call can be made following exactly the same procedure, except that the key word or *pro word* instead of mayday is *PAN PAN, PAN PAN, PAN PAN*. The word MAYDAY is not used.

If there is a medical emergency on board which is serious and needs immediate treatment and you need advice on what to do, or need the crewmember to be taken off ashore as fast as possible then the PAN PAN call is changed to *PAN PAN MEDICO, PAN PAN MEDICO, PAN PAN MEDICO.*

What if the VHF set itself has been damaged? Well, the next way of trying to summon help is by using flares.

Pyrotechnics
There are three basic types of flares: Hand-Held, Smoke and Parachute Rocket.

Hand-held flares These emit either a brilliant red light with a lot of smoke, signalling distress, or a brilliant white light to warn an approaching ship of your presence at night. Note, a white flare is not meant as a distress flare.

Smoke canisters These emit dense clouds of yellow or orange smoke and are dropped in the water beside the vessel, downwind. They are for use in daylight and are particularly helpful when a rescue vessel is nearby but cannot see you.

Parachute flares These are the ones that shoot up into the sky and then drift slowly down giving off a bright red light.

As competent crew we must know how to set them off. Unfortunately the mechanism by which each is fired varies from one pyrotechnic to the other, so there is no substitute for getting hold of them and carefully reading the instructions. As a means of summoning assistance, they are not particularly effective. The amount of time a flare stays lit is remarkably short and so someone has to be looking in your direction at exactly the right time. The only flares with any substantial visual range are the parachute ones.

There is no point in having a fireworks party if there is no one to see you, so the timing of setting off flares is critical. It makes good sense with the parachute flares to send two off, the second about two minutes after the first. If someone is walking along a cliff path, or sailing along the coast, and thinks they see a red flare they are unlikely to dial 999 or call the coastguards on the VHF for fear of being a nuisance. But they will keep looking, and if they then see a second flare, will be convinced enough to call.

Our skipper has watched, with a certain amount of nervous apprehension, as his expensive flares have been passed round the crew; and he has watched hawk-eyed as the firing mechanisms have been looked at in the cockpit and not down below. He has run through the VHF procedure, but in any event he has a waterproof card stuck up beside the radio setting out how the messages are to be sent out, and now listens to the 1350 forecast. Nothing to worry about in the next twenty-four hours and the low doesn't seem to be on the move so he decides to take a chance and head further west.

Here we go again, ropes and sails, ropes and sails.

16
NIGHT SAILING

Our passage to Falmouth passes uneventfully, despite our desire to have an excuse to set a flare off just to see what one looks like, until as we approach Falmouth harbour we encounter a problem not faced so far. Up until now we have spent most of the time sailing on our own but it is clear that we are not the only vessel heading for harbour. Over to our port (left) is a very large commercial vessel also heading towards Falmouth, only it seems to be heading towards us at the same time. The skipper asks us to keep an eye on it whilst he fetches the hand-bearing compass.

It is surprisingly difficult to work out just by looking at it, whether the ship is going to pass ahead of us or behind us or hit us. The only thing we are sure about is that it is getting closer. The skipper asks the helmsman to steer a very steady course, takes a bearing of the ship using the hand bearing-compass, waits for a few more minutes and takes another. The bearing has not changed and so the skipper calls for us to come hard up into the wind and sail closehauled. Our course alters by a good forty degrees and we are now clearly pointing behind the stern of the coaster.

Collision Regulations

In order to govern the behaviour of ships at sea, who gives way and who has right of way, an internationally agreed set of rules has been drawn up that all skippers have to follow, whether small yachts or large tankers. The full title of the rules is the *International Regulations for Preventing Collisions at Sea*, but they are known generally as the Collision Regulations. Although in our situation it is a matter of common sense that we do not sail in front of a fast moving commercial ship, especially as we are not that conspicuous from the bridge of such vessels, there are many occasions when the situation is not so clear cut. And given the number of yachts and small craft about, it makes sense to have a highway code that we can all follow. It is regrettable, but unfortunately true, that quite a few skippers are a bit hazy about the rules and trust to luck; and so no matter what, as the regulations themselves state, it is every skipper's job to try and avoid a collision, even if it means breaking the rules in an emergency.

The rules cover everything from who has right of way to what lights should be carried and how far these lights should be visible, what sound signals should be made in fog – the rules are pretty comprehensive. None of the rules work unless everyone watches where they are going, hence the importance attached to keeping a good lookout at all times. As competent crew we are not expected to know the rules, but we can certainly keep a good look out and tell the skipper of any approaching vessels. In the case of the commercial vessel not only did it have right of way but we needed to show the person on the bridge, if he had seen us, that we were clearly altering course and so there could be no possibility of confusion.

Our skipper endeavours to explain to us some of the basic rules about who has right of way, but it does seem a bit confusing as we have to work out whether other yachts are on port or starboard tacks.

Boats Under Sail

Boats going the same way With two boats sailing in the same direction with the wind coming over the same side of both boats, the boat that the wind hits first, the one closest to the wind, has to give way to the other boat. This makes more sense if you think of two boats sailing along a coast with the wind blowing towards the shore. The one closest to the shore, and therefore closest to danger has the right of way. The skipper of the boat further out to sea has to give way if the boat nearer the shore needs to sail a bit further away from the shore line. If they were both sailing west with the wind oncoming over their left hand or port sides, both would be on port tack. If they were sailing east, with the wind coming over their right hand sides then they would both be on starboard tacks. But whichever boat was closest to the shore, that boat would have the right of way.

Boats going in opposite directions If one boat were sailing west on the port tack, and the other east on the starboard tack, then if they didn't want to hit head on, someone would have to give way. The boat on the port tack, that is with the wind coming over the left hand side of the boat, is the one to give way. The boat on the starboard tack has right of way, and this is why in tight situations a skipper may decide to yell *starboard!* alerting the skipper of the other boat or boats that he expects to be given right of way. This rule applies to boats that are converging diagonally as well as head on.

Boats Under Power

When the yacht's engine goes on, it becomes a *power driven vessel* as far

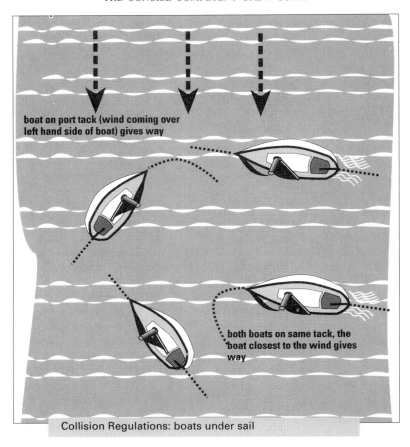

boat on port tack (wind coming over left hand side of boat) gives way

both boats on same tack, the boat closest to the wind gives way

Collision Regulations: boats under sail

as the rules are concerned, even though the sails may still be up. And if two power driven vessels are approaching each other head on, they are both to turn to the right or starboard. If they are approaching diagonally, then only one turns to the right and goes behind the other, the one that has the other vessel on its right hand side.

Boats Overtaking

Driving along a motorway, it is always a delight to have some lunatic drive right up the back of your car, flashing his lights and expecting you to get out of his way immediately. At sea the rule is quite clear: the vessel that is overtaking, whether under power or sail, keeps out of the way of the craft being overtaken. This may be overriden by other rules, which prevent ludicrous situations arising whereby a small yacht would expect to have right of way over a ferry or supertanker.

Our sail progresses without further event and we enter the Fal Estuary and proceed gently under sail past the town of Falmouth and on up to the marina. We are not the only ones here however and have to moor up alongside another yacht. After we have tidied up on board and before we go ashore our skipper reminds us yet again of our obligation to walk round the front of the inside yacht when going ashore, not through the cockpit, and to be lightfooted and quiet. As dusk falls, he unships the ensign and in the back of the cockpit, furls it up and contemplates the next day's passage.

Morning sees us taking on water and fuel – more rope handling as we go to the fuelling pontoon – and then gently motoring out against the tide. Once clear of the moorings, we hoist sail and head off for our chosen lunchtime anchorage, all in high spirits, apart from the skipper who missed the weather forecast while we were messing about getting the fuel. At least the new oil filter isn't leaking.

But he nearly chokes on his sandwich when he hears the 1355 forecast. The low has deepened and speeded up and is heading rapidly towards southern Ireland as the high drifts away to the northeast. The area forecast is 'SW 3/4 increasing 5/6 perhaps 7 later in far southwest' and the coastal weather stations to the west are already recording a fall in barometric pressure and force 4 winds from the southwest.

The skipper decides that, as the passage should take no more than twelve hours, if we leave promptly we should be able to make Plymouth before the weather turns really unpleasant. While he gets out the passage chart, we are asked to look up the tides in the almanac for the next twenty-four hours. And while he plots the passage he asks us to look at the chart for the entrance to Plymouth Sound and to write down on a pad all the lights we should see as we approach from the West; and not just what colour they are, but how they flash, and which ones should we see first, and which ones are the most important to find our way into harbour, such as the lights on the ends of the breakwater. He asks us to look in particular for leading lights.

Passage planning done, we get ourselves and the boat ready. The skipper puts up one of the lee cloths down below and we pile up the extra clothes we might need later on this bunk. We find our safety harnesses and each

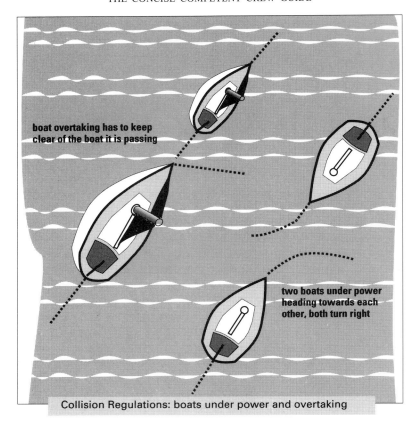

boat overtaking has to keep
clear of the boat it is passing

two boats under power
heading towards each
other, both turn right

Collision Regulations: boats under power and overtaking

stow them separately ready for use later. The galley is sorted out and the packets of soup, biscuits and everything we might need in order to make a quick drink are all brought to the front of the cupboard. The skipper takes a last quick look round to make sure there is nothing loose that could fly out later, and we are ready.

At present the breeze is still a gentle one from the south, and in order not to waste time we motorsail out of the estuary before hoisting full main and genoa and getting ourselves set on course. For a while we just drift gently along at about 3 knots but within a few hours the wind freshens and is beginning to move round more to the south. Soon we are tramping along on a very broad reach, the boat is fairly flying with a white bow wave and we are now up to 6 knots.

The skipper, much to our disgust, decides it is time to reef, just as we are really enjoying ourselves; and he decides to reef the main first. By now we are all in harnesses and the need for them soon becomes apparent. As we turn into the wind in order to put the first reef in, the real strength of the wind is felt. As we had been sailing away from the wind, the true strength had been masked. The motion of the boat is suddenly much more lively and the two crew at the mast have got there on hands and knees. They didn't need to be told to connect their harness straps to the jackstay. The first reef is put in, the sail tidied and we are soon back on course and still making 6 knots.

Within an hour the genoa is changed for the working jib. This time the skipper doesn't turn into the wind but does this with the wind coming over the stern. The din when the sail starts flapping as the sheets are eased off just before it is dropped is amazing; equally amazing, the boat's speed still doesn't reduce.

The wind is gradually creeping more and more round towards the stern and so the skipper rigs up a boom preventer on the main just to be on the safe side, especially as we are not exactly expert helmsmen as yet. As we take turn and turn about on the helm steering a compass course, the skipper plots our position on the chart at regular intervals and makes us cups of tea. None of us is feeling seasick but nobody is too keen to spend much time down below, just in case.

As dusk approaches, the skipper turns on the ship's lights, asks us not to turn on any lights now down below as a bright light reduces our ability to see at night. And as the dusk turns to darkness we begin to see all sorts of lights, some onshore and some out to sea but it is impossible to tell the distance, they could be very close or far away. The skipper tries to explain what we are looking at, in particular other ships' lights and what we look like to them.

Ships' Lights

In order to help distinguish different types of ship, not just by size but also by what they might be doing, certain shapes are hoisted during the day, and certain combinations of lights shown by night. A ship at anchor during the daylight shows a round ball hoisted at the front of the boat, and by night a white light in the same location; a pilot boat shows a red and white flag during the day and red and white lights at night. What shapes and lights have to be shown, and where they are to be displayed, are all contained in the Collision Regulations. The combinations can be confusing both to learn and to spot at sea. Practically all ships and yachts on the move at night, no matter what else they might be showing, have to have their basic navigation lights on; and these are easy to learn.

At the front are shown red and green, at the stern, white; and if the vessel is under power, another white light facing forwards. Look at the diagram to see how they are displayed. Remember the lateral buoys (red on the left, green on the right, as you come in from the sea)? A ship's navigation lights have red on the port (left), green on the starboard (right), just the same. One way of remembering is 'The captain has asked for a drink but there is no red port left'. If we are motor sailing, we are a vessel under power and we need to display the white *steaming* (or motoring) light.

Note that the lights do not shine all round but only cover certain arcs or sectors. This is important because in the dark it is only by observing the red, green and white stern lights that we can work out whether a vessel is coming towards us, crossing in front of us from right to left, or left to right, or going away; and in the case of the steaming light, whether or not it is under sail or under engine. And we need to know all of this in order to work out what we should be doing under the Collision Regulations. When there is a lot of commercial shipping about, mixed up with smaller craft, such as near a busy harbour, our skipper has to have his wits about him to work out what he is looking at and what he should be doing. It is invaluable in such circumstances to have crew that can pick out ships' lights and then be able to say in which direction they think the vessel is moving.

Picking out the red and green lights is no easy matter. On yachts they may be displayed on the top of the mast and in any sort of sea the yacht mast is yawing about and so one minute you may see red, next green, then red, if the yacht is coming towards you. With commercial shipping they are usually showing so many lights, many of them cabin lights through portholes, it is difficult to find the ones you are looking for. The red and green lights do not have to be displayed right at the front, in fact on a container vessel for example they may be situated high up on the sides of the accommodation towards the back of the vessel. However they are always sectored so if you see a red navigation light, you are looking at the port side; a green navigation light, the starboard. (See inside front and back covers for some examples of lights displayed on different craft.)

We can see the white light of Eddystone sweeping the horizon and the skipper does a quick check with the hand-bearing compass on this and crosses it with another bearing taken from the light of a tower on shore. He is distracted when plotting as a gust of wind, much stronger than the overall

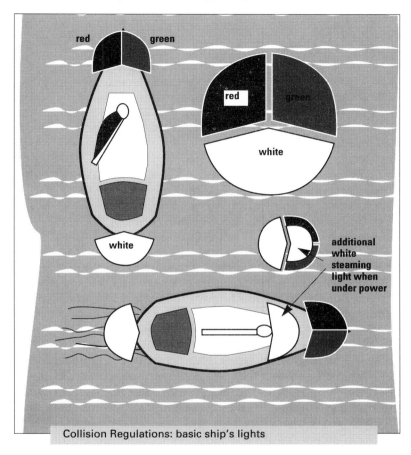

Collision Regulations: basic ship's lights

wind, heels the boat over a bit further and the helmsman finds he is thrown off course by the boat trying to turn up towards the wind. Despite being only within an hour or so from the shelter of the harbour, the skipper decides to put in the second reef. The thought of leaving the safety of the cockpit is not an appealing one. The skipper decides not to risk sheeting the main in hard and reefing while still going down wind, just in case another gust comes through and heels the boat even further over, and so yet again we head up into the wind. Again the increase in noise and wind is quite dramatic; but at least we have the business of reefing sorted out now and the crew that go forward to the mast are not out of the cockpit long.

As we come abeam of Rame Head and see the lights of Plymouth Harbour, the wind is definitely on the increase and the boat swoops down the waves and up on the crests; at night everything seems a bit more dramatic. Looking for the buoys to help the skipper into harbour as soon as possible seems a good idea. At first all is chaos but gradually a pattern of lights emerges, although there are many disagreements along the lines of whether the red light is flashing three every five seconds or five every eight seconds. The problem is that as we go up and down, so does the buoy and sometimes it is lost to view. Once round Rame Head and past the breakwater the seas drop, the winds start to become much much lighter, but the buoys are no easier to spot as they cannot be seen against the background shorelights.

The skipper decides enough is enough for one night, and we don't disagree. We head inshore to find a sheltered anchorage, in fact the same anchorage we started at, only now distance is completely distorted. The lights of the shore look so close and yet they do not seem to be getting any closer as we motorsail slowly towards the coast watching the echo-sounder. We anchor just on highwater in 10 metres, drop the main, put up the anchor light, check our bearings to make sure we are not dragging, and retire for a well earned mug of soup.

What a fantastic trip; normal daily routine will never seem the same again. The adrenalin is still pumping neat.

But why is the skipper already fast asleep propped up in the cabin corner? After all, he hasn't had to do any of the hard work; he has spent most of the trip plotting at the chart table, muttering to himself about weather forecasters, and making cups of tea for us all. He has been in the warm most of the time.

17
QUESTIONS AND ANSWERS

Chapter 1

Look at the diagram and write in as many of the names as you can
remember. The ones you get wrong or can't place are the ones to learn.

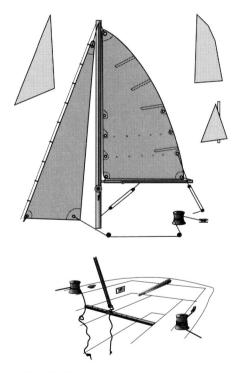

(Answers on pages 8 and 14)

Chapter 2

Get out the string and practise the eight basic knots which are ? (Answers
pages 22 – 31)

Chapters 3 & 4

1 Write out the sequence for taking a jib out of the cockpit locker and hoisting it and note those actions you forget. At sea this could mean the sail bag disappearing over the side.

2 Which knots do you use at either end of the jib/genoa sheets? (Answers page 38/39)

3 Write out the sequence for hoisting the main. Which ropes get tightened and which eased off and in what order? (Answers pages 44/45)

Chapter 5

1 Draw a circle using a saucer. Put the wind blowing down the page from top to bottom. Now, imagine you are in a boat at the centre of the circle pointing towards the wind. Draw in the segment of the circle that a boat cannot sail towards.

2 Now put in the following points of sailing on both tacks, close hauled, beam reach, broad reach and finally running.

(Answer page 53)

3 If the helmsman says *Lee-Oh* what are you expected to do?

4 If the helmsman says *stand by to gybe* what are you expected to do? (Answers pages 54 – 58)

Chapter 6

Write out the sequence for reefing the main from the point the decision is made to reef. (Don't forget the most important action which is to clip what on to where before you leave the cockpit?) (Answers pages 63 – 65)

Chapter 7

Name three main anchors and their advantages and disadvantages. (Answers pages 68 – 74)

What does flaking out the chain mean? (Answer page 76)

Chapter 8

1 Draw a boat alongside a pontoon as viewed from a helicopter. Now add the fenders, the bow and stern lines and the springs.

2 What knots can be used for tying on the fenders? (Answers pages 79 – 81)

3 Does a rope under load come from the bottom of a cleat with the other rope on top or the other way round? (See diagram page 36)

Chapter 9

Draw a square. Is it latitude or longitude up the side? (Answer page 91)

Chapter 10

A compass points to true north. Yes or no? (See diagram page 98)

Chapter 11

1 Why is gas so dangerous on a boat? (Answer page 107)
2 When would you expect to wear a lifejacket? (Answer page 106)

Chapter 12

1 There are two main types of buoyage, what are they?
2 Draw a circle. Put a rock in the middle. Now put four buoys round the edge of the circle, write down their colours and their light characteristics. (Answers pages 113 – 117)

Chapter 13

1 There are two types of weather systems. What are they?(and I don't mean good and bad or wet and dry).
2 Which way does the wind blow in these systems? (Answers pages 122/123)

Chapter 14

What are the main components of a diesel engine? (Answer page 132)

Chapter 15

You have to send a mayday by VHF. What should you say? (Answer page 142)

Chapter 16

1 Two sailing boats heading towards each other. How do you work out which has priority and which has to alter course?
2 Two power boats heading towards each other head on. Which way should each one turn? (Answers pages 145 – 148)

Introduction

What is the point of going sailing?   ANSWER - TO HAVE FUN!

Appendix 1
TYPES OF BOAT AND HULL

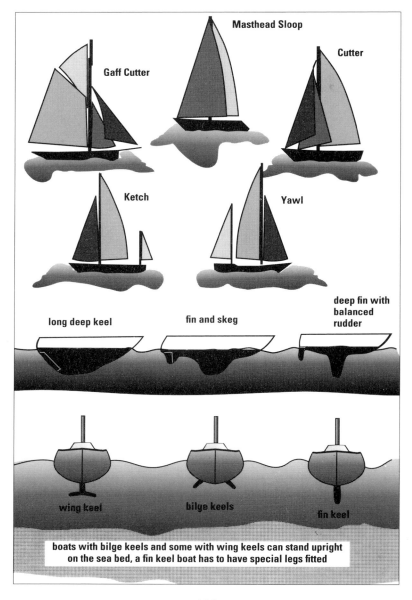

Masthead Sloop

Cutter

Gaff Cutter

Ketch

Yawl

deep fin with balanced rudder

long deep keel

fin and skeg

wing keel

bilge keels

fin keel

boats with bilge keels and some with wing keels can stand upright on the sea bed, a fin keel boat has to have special legs fitted

Appendix 2
RYA COURSE STRUCTURE

Course	Suggested minimum pre-course experience	Assumed knowledge	Course content	Ability after course
Competent Crew practical	None	None	Basic seamanship & helmsmanship	Useful crew member
Day Skipper shorebased	Some practical experience desirable	None	Basic seamanship & introduction to navigation & meteorology	
Day Skipper practical	5 days 100 miles 4 night hours	Basic navigation & sailing ability	Basic pilotage, boat handling, seamanship & navigation	Skipper a small yacht in familiar waters by day
Coastal Skipper/ Yachtmaster Offshore shore-based		Navigation to Day Skipper shorebased standard	Offshore & coastal navigation, pilotage & meteorology	
Coastal Skipper practical	15 days (2 days as skipper) 300 miles 8 night hours	Navigation to Coastal Skipper shorebased standard. Sailing to Day Skipper practical standard	Skippering techniques for coastal & offshore passages	Skipper a yacht on coastal passages by day & night
Yachtmaster Ocean shore-based	Coastal and offshore sailing	Navigation to Coastal Skipper & Yachtmaster Offshore shorebased standard	Astro-navigation, ocean meteorology & passage planning	

*Course requirements are subject to change

157

Index